JUST FOOD

Phil Vickery

JUST FOOD

Phil Vickery

With photographs by
Georgia Glynn Smith

HEADLINE

For Grandma Billington

First published in 1999
by HEADLINE BOOK PUBLISHING

10 9 8 7 6 5 4 3 2 1

British Library Cataloguing in Publication Data

Vickery, Phil
Just Food
1. Cookery
I. Title
641.5

ISBN 0 7472 7406 1

Recipe home economist: Julia Alger
Photography home economist: Maxine Clarke
Stylist: Penny Markham
Design: Ben Cracknell
Keying: Letterpart Limited, Reigate, Surrey

Printed and bound in Great Britain by
Butler and Tanner Ltd, Frome and London

HEADLINE BOOK PUBLISHING
A division of Hodder Headline PLC
338 Euston Road
London NW1 3BH

www.headline.co.uk
www.hodderheadline.com

Acknowledgements

My thanks to all the people from whom I have hijacked recipes – Mum and Dad, Gerry, Ben, Paul, Mike and all the lads. Thanks also to all at Headline, especially Heather for persevering with the original plan, and Lindsay and Jo for not hassling me too much. Special thanks go to Georgia for some of the best food photos I've ever seen.

Also to my dog Max, for barking at me to get out into the fresh air where I can think more logically (and to Sue for looking after him while I'm away); Kit, Louise and Gill for their unswerving kindness, guidance and support through some very difficult times; Julia for not chucking in the towel when I was in Shetland and for doing a sterling job in being able to decipher my scribble.

And finally, to Fern, not just for the use of the kitchen to cook and eat a lot of the dishes but for being the most important person in my life . . . thanks.

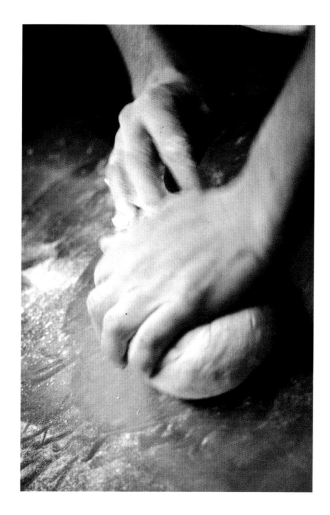

Contents

Introduction

I have always been interested in food, ever since I was a small child. Some of my earliest memories involve my grandmother making delicious fruit pies using old Fray Bentos tins, and eating her home-made toffee. Parkin was another speciality. My mum carried on the tradition and is also a very good cook, and my father makes fantastic stews and broths. This kind of great British grub – black pudding, custard pies, fish and chips – is the type of food I find myself returning to again and again.

At college, my interest in cooking took a back seat for a while after beer and football and other typical student distractions. My main criteria when it came to food then were that it had to be cheap, simple to make and filling enough to soak up the obligatory vast quantities of alcohol. Yet that's not to say that I didn't eat well, even if it wasn't the sort of food you'd see on a restaurant menu. Heinz baked beans, chilli con carne or even bananas and custard are all delicious, quick and easy – *real* comfort food at its best. I don't know anyone who doesn't secretly still love this kind of student fare. Some great flavour combinations used to come from late-night raids on the store cupboard: baked beans and grated cheese; pickled onion, ham and crisp sandwiches and even peanut butter and pickle on toast. I admit I've eaten all of these and would happily do so again. Escoffier would turn in his grave.

When I first became a professional chef, I fell into the common trap of cooking some dishes merely to gain credibility – a type of food snobbery which made me feel both pressured and constrained. Thankfully, now I just cook what I really want to eat. Although I will always dedicate huge amounts of time to perfecting combinations, tastes and textures, I'm a great believer in having fun with cooking, making what we *really* want and not necessarily what we think we ought to. Two of my all-time favourite dishes are steamed steak and kidney pudding with mash, mushy peas and gravy followed by a

really basic trifle – angel cake soaked in custard and chilled – mmm! They're just so good and easy. Many chefs these days look too far afield instead of enjoying what's right in front of them.

I came to the Castle via Gravetye Manor in East Grinstead, West Sussex. The owner, Peter Herbert, instilled in me the passion not only for great home-grown produce but also for perfection and quality. I still think it's the best-run country house hotel in Britain with some of the best service I've ever seen. In 1990, I moved to the Castle Hotel restaurant in Taunton, Somerset, taking over the reins from Gary Rhodes. I have been there ever since, to carry on the Castle tradition of great British food, first started by Chris Oakes then continued by Rhodes. The Castle's offshoot, Brazz, came about when we decided to refurbish the old pub next door. Rather than have another pub we thought we'd try to create a modern café, brasserie and bar. It was a bit of a gamble but it's worked so well since it opened in 1998 that we plan to open a few more.

I have been cooking professionally now for the best part of 20 years, yet I'm still a great believer in serving food as simply as possible, both in the restaurant and at home. It's essential to use the best raw produce available. I try to buy organic whenever I can, but due to the size of the Castle and the amount of food I need to buy on a regular basis it's not always possible. Having said that I do try to find local people to rear or grow certain things organically. I use supermarkets as much as sources of inspiration as anything else – the number of new lines they stock these days is fantastic and I always leave bursting with ideas.

Food is all about experimentation and good old common sense. Certain classic combinations always work well: pears and chocolate, orange and chocolate, lamb and mint sauce (the French hate the idea), pork and apples, lobster and chicken, to name just a few. But occasionally you come across a new one, quite by accident – peas, pasta and horseradish for instance works brilliantly (see page 54). Trying out new ideas can be hit and miss but it's great fun and when something works it's enormously satisfying. Use the recipes in this book as guidelines, rather than rigid formulas – let your imagination do the rest. Timings for all the recipes are accurate, but use your head and if you see something cooking too quickly then turn down the heat. Take short cuts by all means, so long as they're not detrimental to the end result. Similarly, if you want a little more or less of a particular ingredient then go for it – though be careful of certain recipes, such as those for pastry, bread or desserts, which will need very careful measuring or they won't work. But again why not experiment with other items? Do your own thing.

Just Food is a collection of my favourite recipes, the kind of food I cook regularly at home. It is written for real people leading busy lives, who enjoy entertaining but don't like sleepless nights followed by hours in the kitchen. A lot of the dishes here are from the days when money was tight and I had to cook using only what was in the cupboard, but that doesn't mean the end result has to taste cheap. Above all, I have tried to make these recipes as easy-to-follow as possible. It's not a professional tome full of fancy chef techniques, nor is it a quick cookbook which sacrifices flavour for the sake of saving an extra few minutes in the kitchen. Instead, *Just Food* is all about simple meals, cooked carefully using the best ingredients available, with recipes I have used over the years. I hope you enjoy them.

Phil Vickery

Brunch

Quick Crab Kedgeree with Parsley Butter

Serves 4

Kedgeree is a marvellous dish and an old English favourite. This quick and easy version will make a tasty snack at any time of the day. You can substitute the crab with prawns or salmon. A culinary tip: frozen rice that you can cook in the microwave is fantastic – I've got several packets in my freezer at home and after a long day it's so quick to heat through.

350g (12 oz) white crab meat, fresh or frozen

115g (4 oz) butter, melted

225g (8 oz) baby button mushrooms, cut in half

3 × 200g (7 oz) sachets frozen rice, defrosted

1 tbsp vegetable oil

3 tbsp roughly chopped fresh parsley

4 spring onions, chopped

salt and freshly ground black pepper

- If using frozen crab, defrost following the packet instructions.

- Pour a quarter of the butter into a wok or large frying pan and heat until beginning to foam. Add the mushrooms and cook for about 3 minutes, until starting to soften. Remove the mushrooms from the pan and keep warm.

- Place the rice in the wok and heat through (if you need to, add a little vegetable oil to keep the grains separate). This should only take a few minutes. Add the crab meat, parsley, spring onions, mushrooms and the remaining melted butter and stir gently to combine and warm through. Do not let the crab overcook. Serve straightaway.

Bubble and Squeak with Poached Eggs and Really Easy Hollandaise

Serves 4

The best thing about Christmas is Boxing Day brunch: turkey sandwiches, fried stuffing with bubble and squeak made from the leftover Brussels sprouts, and the exquisite and flavoursome turkey and barley broth. I've spent many a Boxing Day enjoying flasks of broth, crusty bread and Christmas cake, thankful that it's all over for another year! So, if you are too tired to move, nursing a hangover or just plain fed up with it all, then try this delicious bubble and squeak.

4 tbsp olive oil

2 onions, sliced

1 tsp chopped fresh marjoram, optional

280g (10 oz) cooked Brussels sprouts, chopped, or cooked cabbage, shredded

450g (1 lb) warm, plain mashed potato – with no cream, milk or butter added

salt and freshly ground black pepper

25g (1 oz) dried breadcrumbs

flour, to dust

50–75ml (2–2½ fl oz) vinegar or lemon juice

4 eggs

For the hollandaise sauce

50ml (2 fl oz) white wine vinegar

50ml (2 fl oz) white wine, or water

1 tsp crushed white peppercorns

175g (6 oz) unsalted butter

4 egg yolks

½ lemon

pinch of caster sugar

- Heat 2 tablespoons of the olive oil in a frying pan. Add the onions and cook gently for a few minutes until softened, but do not allow to brown. Cool slightly.

- Stir in the marjoram, if using, then add the onions and sprouts to the mashed potato and season well. If the mixture is too wet, add a few breadcrumbs to make a fairly stiff dough. Shape the mixture into balls about the size of a small orange, then flatten out and allow to chill while you make the sauce.

- The secret of this hollandaise is that the butter must be bubbling when it is added to the egg yolks – if it is not hot enough the sauce will not thicken sufficiently. In a pan, heat the vinegar and wine or water with the peppercorns, bring to the boil and simmer rapidly until the liquid has reduced by half to 50ml (2 fl oz). Strain out the peppercorns then return the liquid to the pan and bring back to the boil.

- Meanwhile, in another pan gently melt the butter. Add the reduced liquid and bring to a rolling boil. Place the egg yolks in a liquidizer and blitz, then with the motor running slowly pour the hot vinegar and butter mixture into the liquidizer in a thin stream through the lid. Pour the sauce into a bowl and leave for 3 minutes, stirring occasionally. If the sauce has not thickened enough, pour it back into the pan and stir constantly over the lowest possible heat until it thickens. Taste the sauce and adjust the seasoning, adding a squeeze of lemon juice and a pinch of sugar if necessary. Keep warm.

- Heat the remaining olive oil in a frying pan. Dust both sides of the patties in flour, then add to the frying pan and cook for a few minutes on each side until golden brown.

- To make the poached eggs, fill a medium-sized pan with cold water and add the vinegar or lemon juice (I also add a pinch of salt to the water as I think it helps to coagulate the egg white). Bring the pan to the boil and, when the water is bubbling, crack in the eggs. Bring the water back to simmering point, then reduce the heat and simmer gently for 2–3 minutes, or until the eggs are just set and still a little soft. Carefully remove from the water using a slotted spoon and drain on kitchen paper.

- Place the potato cakes on serving plates, sit an egg on top of each and spoon over the sauce. Serve with crusty bread.

Griddled Flat Mushrooms with Black Pudding and Parsley & Garlic Bread

Serves 4

A lot of chefs cook button mushrooms for breakfast but I don't think they have any flavour and prefer to use flat or open cap mushrooms – they're often a bit cheaper too. When grilled they seem to take on an almost meaty texture, provided you don't overcook them. Flat field mushrooms are even nicer but tend to contain a lot of extra water, so they are best 'flash-fried' in very hot oil and finished in a little butter.

225g (8 oz) unsalted butter, softened

2 cloves garlic, crushed

2 heaped tbsp roughly chopped fresh flat leaf parsley

$\frac{1}{2}$ lemon

salt and freshly ground black pepper

2 French bread baguettes

8 medium flat mushrooms

1 tbsp olive oil

1 medium ring good quality black pudding, about 450g (1 lb)

4 medium slices bread, crusts removed

- Preheat the oven to 220°C/425°F/Gas 7 and preheat the grill to high.

- Mix together the butter, garlic and parsley until well incorporated then add a squeeze of lemon juice, season and mix again (I like the butter to taste fairly peppery). Reserve about 85g (3 oz) of the butter mixture.

- Cut the baguettes in half lengthways then in half again crosswise and spread the remaining butter over the cut surfaces. Place the baguettes on a baking sheet and bake in the oven for about 8–10 minutes, or until browned.

- Remove the stalks from the mushrooms and brush over their surfaces with a pastry brush to remove any loose dirt (there is no need to wash domestic mushrooms as they are grown in sterile conditions). Place the mushrooms on a baking sheet, gills upwards, drizzle over the olive oil and season well. Place the mushrooms under the grill and cook for 5–6 minutes, or until just tender. Do not overcook. Leave the mushrooms on the baking sheet, but remove from the grill and keep warm.

- Cut the black pudding into thin slices on an angle.

- Heat the reserved garlic butter in a large frying pan until the butter is beginning to foam. Add the black pudding and cook for 2–3 minutes on each side, or until the black pudding just begins to fall apart slightly. Be careful that the butter does not burn.

- Meanwhile, blitz the sliced bread in a food processor to make breadcrumbs.

- When the garlic baguettes are nice and crispy around the edges, remove them from the oven and keep warm.

- Arrange the slices of black pudding on the mushrooms, spoon over any remaining butter from the pan, season the breadcrumbs and sprinkle over the top. Place the baking sheet back under the grill, reduce the heat slightly and cook for a few minutes, until the breadcrumbs are golden brown.

- Serve the mushrooms with the garlic baguettes and top the mushrooms with fried eggs if you want to go the whole hog.

Bacon and Sweetcorn Fritters with Fried Eggs

Serves 4

Fried eggs are wonderful when they're cooked properly; the secret is to season them well with salt and pepper. I know the health gurus tell us that fried eggs are bad for us and that we should switch to poaching, but hey, once in a while is fine. Just remember – it's gluttony that kills man, not food! This is a perfect summer brunch dish.

For the batter:

2 eggs and 1 egg white
100g (3½ oz) plain flour, sieved
about 75ml (2½ fl oz) milk
salt and freshly ground black pepper

4–6 rashers smoked, rindless back bacon
198g can sweetcorn niblets, drained
2 small shallots, finely chopped
pinch of ground cumin
1 tbsp chopped chives
vegetable oil, for frying
4 large eggs
salt and freshly ground black pepper

- To make the batter, place the egg white in a large bowl and crack one of the whole eggs into another bowl. Separate the remaining egg, adding the yolk to the bowl with the whole egg and the white to the bowl containing the white. Add the flour and about 50ml (2 fl oz) of the milk to the whole egg and extra yolk and mix together (this should stop you getting a lumpy batter). Gradually add enough of the remaining milk to make a thick batter – you don't want it too thin or it will run everywhere. Season the batter well with salt and pepper and allow to stand for about 20 minutes – this allows the batter to settle. It may thicken up slightly, in which case add a little more milk.

- Meanwhile, preheat the grill and cook the bacon on both sides until crisp. Allow to cool slightly then cut it into small pieces.

- Tip the sweetcorn into a colander and use the back of a spoon to gently squeeze out any excess water. Add the sweetcorn to the batter, together with the shallots, bacon, cumin and chives. Whisk the egg whites until stiff, then add them to the batter and fold together.

- Heat a little vegetable oil in a non-stick frying pan. Add spoonfuls of the batter mixture and allow it to spread slightly. Cook the fritters over a medium heat for about 2–3 minutes, or until just set and golden brown on the base. Turn them over and cook the other side. Continue until all the mixture is used up.

- Meanwhile, heat some more vegetable oil in a separate frying pan, crack in the remaining eggs and fry to taste. Spoon a little of the oil over the yolks as the eggs are cooking, to set them. Season the eggs well – this adds a wonderful flavour.

- To serve, arrange the fritters on hot plates and top with one or two fried eggs – HP sauce is the only accompaniment you'll need.

Oven-baked Eggs with Tomato Relish and Gruyère Cheese

Serves 4

To me, tomatoes and eggs are a great combination. At breakfast in the hotel we always serve grilled tomatoes with eggs cooked every way possible. Here, the pungent, full tomato flavour is contrasted with the richness of the egg yolks, topped with melting cheese, to make a delicious breakfast special.

2 tbsp olive oil

1 small onion, finely chopped

1 clove garlic, crushed

2 tsp chopped basil

400g (14 oz) can chopped tomatoes

1 tsp tomato purée

1 tsp caster sugar

1 tsp white wine vinegar

salt and freshly ground black pepper

4 eggs

55g (2 oz) Gruyère cheese, grated

- Preheat the oven to 220°C/425°F/Gas 7.

- Heat the oil in a pan. Add the onion and garlic and cook on a low heat for 5–6 minutes, stirring so that the onion softens without colouring. Stir in the basil, tomatoes and tomato purée, then simmer uncovered for about 35 minutes, or until the tomato mixture has thickened. Add the sugar and vinegar and season (you may want to add an extra dash of olive oil to finish the relish). Allow to cool, then pour into a small ovenproof dish, large enough to take the four eggs, or four ramekin dishes. Use a spoon to make four small 'nests' in the relish. (You could prepare this in advance, if required.)

- Place the dish or ramekins on a baking sheet, crack an egg into each hollow in the relish and season well. Bake in the oven for about 10–12 minutes, or until the eggs are just beginning to set. Remove the dish from the oven and scatter some of the cheese over each egg. Return to the oven and cook for a couple of minutes until the cheese has melted. Serve immediately.

Creamy Kipper Mash with Spring Onions and Garlic Bread

Serves 4

Lots of people don't care for kippers, but I think they're wonderful. Try and get natural smoked kippers if you can – they are so much nicer than the commercially dyed variety; Manx kippers are the best in my opinion. I can remember my father having kippers for breakfast when I was a child, and Mum complaining for the rest of the week about the cooking smells in the house. She tells me that this is not a problem any more, thanks to the invention of clingfilm.

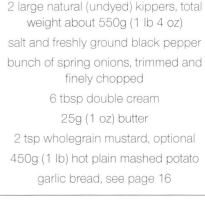

> 2 large natural (undyed) kippers, total weight about 550g (1 lb 4 oz)
>
> salt and freshly ground black pepper
>
> bunch of spring onions, trimmed and finely chopped
>
> 6 tbsp double cream
>
> 25g (1 oz) butter
>
> 2 tsp wholegrain mustard, optional
>
> 450g (1 lb) hot plain mashed potato
>
> garlic bread, see page 16

- Lay the kippers in a deep heatproof dish. They should fit quite snugly. Season, then pour over enough boiling water from a kettle to just cover the fish. Cover straightaway with clingfilm and allow to stand for 20 minutes.

- Meanwhile, stir the spring onions, cream, butter and mustard, if using, into the mashed potato.

- Carefully pour the hot water off the kippers. Remove the middle bone from the fish then take out all the other bones – they should come out very easily. Gently peel off the skin and flake the flesh.

- Fold the flakes of kipper into the hot mash and season. Divide the mash between warm plates, and serve with hot garlic and parsley bread. You could even serve poached eggs on top to make a more substantial brunch dish.

Crushed Raspberries with Oats and Double Cream

Serves 4

This makes an ideal summer breakfast. Alternatively, serve in a glass with shortbread as dessert at lunch or dinner. I use half-thawed frozen raspberries for this dish. They start to break down when folded into the cream, which gives a pleasing visual effect.

350ml (12 fl oz) double cream

200g (7 oz) tub sheep's yoghurt

140g (5 oz) cooked porridge, chilled overnight then broken up with a fork

about 140g (5 oz) caster sugar

280g (10 oz) frozen raspberries, half-thawed, or you can use fresh

finely grated zest and juice of ½ lemon

2 tbsp runny honey, to serve

- Start by whipping the double cream to soft peaks. In a separate bowl, stir the sheep's yoghurt into the broken-up porridge until smooth then fold the mixture into the whipped cream. Fold in the caster sugar, tasting to check the sweetness.

- Finally, lightly fold in the raspberries and lemon zest, then add the lemon juice to taste. Do not overmix the ingredients – it's nice to see the separate swirls of raspberries and double cream. To finish, drizzle over the honey.

Brunch Bap with Glazed Chicken, Black Pudding, Bacon, Mayo and Beets

Serves 4

Some years ago, I jetted off to Australia and New Zealand for a while. I mostly shot and fished (catching my largest salmon ever – a fraction over 25 lbs), but I also found the best burger bar in the world in Christchurch, New Zealand. Unfortunately I can't remember the name, but it was small, packed with people and very popular. Their special was a burger called 'The Kitchen Sink' which had everything from boiled eggs to sauerkraut in it. It was huge, immensely filling and, very important in those days, cheap. Needless to say, I ate those burgers regularly. Here is my version of the kitchen sink, without the burger.

finely grated zest and juice of 1 lemon

1 tsp ground cumin

2 tbsp olive oil

4 skinless, boneless chicken thighs

1 tsp chopped fresh basil

small clove garlic, crushed

4 tbsp mayonnaise

salt and freshly ground black pepper

2 tbsp vegetable oil

12 slices black pudding

8 rashers smoked streaky bacon

four burger baps, split in half

8 slices pickled beetroot, optional

- Mix the lemon zest and juice with the cumin and olive oil in a non-metallic dish. Add the chicken thighs and turn to coat. Allow to stand at room temperature for 15–20 minutes, the chicken flesh will become opaque.

- Stir the basil and garlic into the mayonnaise and season.

- Heat the vegetable oil in a non-stick frying pan, add the black pudding and cook for about 2–3 minutes on each side. Transfer on to a piece of kitchen paper to drain and keep warm. Add the bacon to the pan and cook on both sides until crisp, then keep warm with the black pudding.

- Use kitchen paper to pat dry the chicken thighs, then cook in the frying pan for about 5 minutes on each side, or until cooked through. Drain on kitchen paper. Meanwhile, toast the cut side of the baps under a hot grill.

- To finish the dish, place the bottom half of the baps on plates, top with layers of chicken, beetroot (if using), bacon and black pudding and spoon over some of the basil and garlic mayonnaise. Top with the bap lids and serve.

Barbecues and Picnics

Andy's Pizza Pane

Makes about 12 mini pizzas

Andy, the head chef in Brazz, makes very good pizza dough. This is his recipe for a delicious garlic and tomato bread which he calls 'Pizza Pane'. Serve it on its own, as an alternative to bread rolls, or as a starter. It also works well served with taramasalata or humous.

For the dough:

500g (1 lb 2 oz) strong white bread flour

75g (2¾ oz) fresh yeast, broken up

15g (½ oz) caster sugar

15g (½ oz) salt

5 tbsp olive oil

For the topping:

4 plum tomatoes

2 cloves garlic, crushed

small bunch of fresh basil, chopped

100ml (3½ fl oz) extra virgin olive oil

salt and freshly ground black pepper

- Place the flour, yeast, sugar and salt in a food mixer (using the dough hook attachment if you have one) and set on a low speed. With the mixer operating, gradually add the olive oil and about 350–400ml (12–14 fl oz) of warm water and mix thoroughly – the dough will eventually work itself away from the sides of the bowl. Once this stage has been reached, continue to mix for a further 5 minutes.

- Remove the dough from the mixer and place in a bowl which has been lightly greased with a little olive oil. Cover with clingfilm and leave to rise in a warm place for about 45 minutes to 1 hour, or until the dough has doubled in size.

- Meanwhile, make the topping. Chop the tomatoes into small pieces and place in a bowl, then mix in the garlic, basil and oil and season well. Allow to stand for at least 1 hour to allow the flavours to infuse and develop. This mixture will keep in a sealed container in the fridge for up to a week.

- When the dough is ready, preheat the oven to 230°C/450°F/Gas 8. Break the dough into twelve pieces, knead each one lightly, then roll out very thinly on a floured surface to make circles, approximately 15cm (6 in) in diameter.

- Prick the dough all over with a fork and place on a baking sheet. Spoon on the topping, making sure that the bases are not flooded by too much oil. Bake for about 10–12 minutes, or until each base is crisp and well risen.

Citrus Chicken Escalopes with Mango Salsa

Serves 4

I really enjoy chicken, especially the leg meat which is juicy and tender when cooked this way. Chicken breast, on the other hand, can be quite tricky to cook on a barbecue, where the fierce heat can dry out and toughen the meat very quickly.

finely grated zest and juice of 1 lemon
and 1 lime

1 clove garlic, crushed

1 tsp caster sugar

1 tsp sesame oil

salt and freshly ground black pepper

8 boneless chicken thighs

For the salsa:

1 large mango

1 red chilli, seeds removed and finely chopped

4 spring onions, chopped

1½ tsp fresh lime juice

1 tbsp olive oil

pinch of caster sugar

1–2 tsp chopped fresh mint

celery salt

25g (1 oz) unsalted butter, softened

- Place the lemon and lime zest and juice in a shallow non-metallic dish, add the garlic, sugar, sesame oil, salt and pepper, then stir to dissolve the sugar.

- Trim any excess fat or skin off the chicken, then add to the marinade and turn to coat. Cover the dish with clingfilm and chill for 4–5 hours, or overnight if possible.

- To make the salsa, stand the mango on its end and, with a sharp knife, cut off the 'cheeks' of flesh from both sides, keeping the knife close to the flat central stone. Peel, then cut the flesh into chunks and place in a bowl with the chilli, spring onions, lime juice, olive oil, caster sugar and mint. Allow to stand so that the flavours infuse.

- When you come to cook the chicken, remove the thighs from the marinade and pat dry using kitchen paper. Season with celery salt and black pepper.

- Smear a little butter over each thigh and place under a preheated conventional grill, or on a hot barbecue. Grill on both sides until thoroughly cooked – depending on the intensity of the heat, this will be about 12–16 minutes in total. Be careful not to burn the chicken.

- Serve when hot and crispy accompanied by plenty of salsa and green salad.

Cory Mattson's Real Southern Fried Chicken

Serves 4

Every summer I try to spend a few days trout fishing. Last year I booked a five-day fishing trip to the Clinch River in Tennessee, USA, with my very good friend Cory Mattson, the talented chef at the Fearington House Hotel, North Carolina. We would start fishing around 4.00 a.m., after feasting on strong coffee and Cory's granola (a sort of muesli). After four or five hours' fishing we were always ravenous and would dive into this chicken dish – the best I've ever eaten.

3 tbsp dried oregano
3 tbsp dried thyme
1½ tbsp ground white pepper
6 tbsp plain flour
1 tsp rock salt
3 eggs
dash of Tabasco sauce
4 chicken legs
vegetable oil, for frying

- Preheat the oven to 200°C/400°F/Gas 6.

- Finely grind the oregano and thyme together using a pestle and mortar, or in a mini food processor, then place in a large plastic bag with the ground white pepper, flour and rock salt and shake to mix.

- In a shallow dish, beat the eggs, together with 100ml (3½ fl oz) of water and the Tabasco.

- Cut the chicken leg in half at the joint to give drumstick and thigh pieces. Add the chicken to the bag containing the flour and spice mixture and shake to dust lightly, then remove from the flour and place on one side. Dip each piece of chicken in the egg mixture, shake off any excess, then put back into the flour mixture to coat – it's best to do this one piece at a time, otherwise you'll get very messy.

- Heat the vegetable oil in a frying pan – there should be enough oil to come halfway up the pieces of chicken. Add the chicken pieces in batches, frying for a few minutes on each side, or until golden brown. Sit a wire cooling rack securely on top of a roasting pan or baking tray, remove the browned chicken from the frying pan and arrange on the wire rack.

- Bake in the oven for about 25 minutes, or until the chicken is cooked through. Remove from the oven and allow to rest for a further 15–20 minutes.

Hot and Spicy Chix Wings with Sweetcorn Mayo

Serves 4

We cook these wings as canapés at the Castle. For the restaurant we trim and bone them so that they look perfect – a job the lads hate with a passion! However, in this recipe they are cooked in a very straightforward way and are excellent for taking on picnics.

900g (2 lb) chicken wings

salt

For the marinade:

2 tbsp vegetable oil

6 tbsp Heinz tomato ketchup

2 tbsp clear honey

2 tsp five spice powder

2 tbsp Worcestershire sauce

2 tbsp dark soy sauce

dash of lemon juice

2 × 198g cans sweetcorn niblets, well drained

200g (7 oz) good quality mayonnaise

1 small red onion, finely chopped

salt and freshly ground black pepper

- Put the chicken wings in a deep pan and pour on enough cold water to cover. Add 1 teaspoon of salt and bring to the boil, then turn down the heat and simmer for about 15–20 minutes. Drain the chicken through a colander and allow to cool.

- Place all the marinade ingredients in a non-metallic bowl and stir together, then add the cooled chicken wings and turn to coat in the marinade. Cover the bowl and allow the chicken to marinate in the fridge overnight, turning occasionally.

- Gently squeeze out any excess moisture from the sweetcorn and stir into the mayonnaise with the onion.

- Do not make the mistake of allowing the barbecue to get too hot – if you do, the chicken wings will burn because of the amount of honey and ketchup in the marinade. Wait until the coals are cooling down before you attempt to cook the wings – they will only take about 5–8 minutes, as they have already been cooked through, so all you are doing is heating them through thoroughly and giving them a nice glaze.

- Serve the glazed wings with the sweetcorn mayonnaise.

Andy's Lamb Chops with Orange and Redcurrant Marinade

Serves 4

finely grated zest and juice of 1 orange

½ tsp English mustard

1 tbsp redcurrant jelly

3 tbsp olive oil

1 sprig fresh rosemary

salt and freshly ground black pepper

4 thick lamb leg steaks, about 125g
(4½ oz) each

Place the orange zest and juice, mustard, jelly, oil and rosemary in a mini food processor and blitz until smooth. Pour the mixture into a non-metallic shallow dish and season with salt. Add the lamb steaks and leave to marinate for at least 2–3 hours, or overnight in the fridge.

Drain off the excess marinade and reserve, then pat the lamb steaks dry with kitchen paper. Season the meat and cook either on a barbecue or in a preheated griddle pan, for about 15 minutes for a rare result, or a few minutes longer if you prefer your meat more well done. Turn the lamb steaks regularly and brush over a little more of the marinade during cooking. Keep a close eye on the chaps – because of the amount of sugar in the jelly, they will brown very quickly.

Lamb's Kidney Skewers with Seed Mustard and Chilli Oil

Serves 4

A lot of people are put off by kidneys – often because they have bad memories of school dinners and the awful, strong pig's liver and kidneys that were served there. Lamb's kidneys, however, are very good to eat, providing you pay a little attention to the details. One of my first tasks as a young commis chef was to peel and de-skin 160 lamb's kidneys – nearly enough to put me off for life. But they are definitely worth the effort and make an unusual barbecue dish. A useful barbecue tip: if you are using wooden skewers, soak them overnight in cold water to stop them burning.

1 small red chilli

3 tbsp olive oil

1 tbsp wholegrain mustard

1 tbsp chopped fresh tarragon

salt and freshly ground black pepper

16 fresh lamb's kidneys

For the dressing:

150g (5½ oz) natural yoghurt

1 tbsp chopped fresh mint

2 pinches freshly grated nutmeg

pinch of caster sugar

- Cut the chilli in half lengthways, carefully scrape out the seeds and discard them. Chop the chilli flesh very finely and add to the olive oil. (You can add more chilli if you want to, but I like to keep the roof of my mouth and my constitution intact!) Mix in the wholegrain mustard, chopped tarragon, a pinch of salt and one turn of the peppermill. Leave to stand for 2–3 hours, turning occasionally.

- Lay the kidneys flat on a chopping board and cut each in half horizontally to give thin pieces. Snip out the cores then thread a few pieces of kidney on to four skewers, exposing the open cut. Thread the skewer in and out of each piece of kidney a couple of times so it doesn't 'flop' too much. Place to one side.

- To make the dressing, mix together the yoghurt, mint, nutmeg and sugar, taste and add a little salt and pepper if you think it needs it.

- Make sure the barbecue is very hot, as kidneys tend to exude a lot of moisture. Brush the kidneys with some of the chilli oil, then seal both sides of the meat as quickly as possible. Cook for about 10 minutes, turning occasionally and brushing over some more of the chilli oil – I like to serve my kidneys nice and pink, but that's up to you.

- Serve on a plate and spoon over the yoghurt dressing.

Ricotta, Fresh Fig and Parma Ham Pastries

Serves 4

1 sheet ready-rolled puff pastry, measuring
about 28 × 23cm (11 × 9 in)

beaten egg, to egg wash

115g (4 oz) ricotta

1 tsp chopped fresh sage

$\frac{1}{2}$ tsp black peppercorns, crushed

salt and freshly ground black pepper

4 slices Parma ham, cut in half lengthways

4 fresh ripe figs, cut in half lengthways

1 tbsp olive oil

● Preheat the oven to 200°C/400°F/Gas 6. Cut the pastry into eight circles 7$\frac{1}{2}$cm (3 in) in diameter. Using a sharp knife, make a cut about halfway through the thickness of the pastry around the edge of each, 5mm ($\frac{1}{4}$ in) away from the edge. Carefully egg wash the surface of the pastry, being careful not to brush egg wash beyond the cut marks, as this will make the pastry rise unevenly. Prick the inner circles with a fork then place on baking sheets and chill for 30 minutes.

● Place the ricotta in a bowl, together with the sage and crushed peppercorns, season with salt and mix together. Wrap the ham slices around the figs.

● Divide the ricotta mixture into eight, then spoon into the centre of each pastry disc and spread out slightly. Sit the wrapped figs, cut side uppermost, in the centre of each disc, drizzle over a little olive oil and season with salt and pepper.

● Cook in the oven for 10–12 minutes, or until the pastry is well risen and golden brown. Remove from the oven and allow to cool for 10 minutes before eating.

Spiced Pork and Prune Patties with Lamb's Lettuce

Pork and prunes are a wonderful combination but I can already hear you saying 'I hate prunes'! Here, though, there's only a small proportion of prunes to a large amount of meat and when they're cooked the patties are delicious – trust me. In this recipe I've used nutmeg and chilli powder, but you can use whatever spices you like – sage and mace go very well together too. Make sure you cook the patties slowly, otherwise they will dry out.

6 ready-to-eat prunes
450g (1 lb) lean pork mince
2 tbsp chopped fresh sage
$\frac{1}{4}$ tsp ground nutmeg
salt and freshly ground black pepper
2 pinches red chilli powder
1 egg, beaten
about 85g (3 oz) lamb's lettuce
$\frac{1}{2}$ lemon
about 1 tbsp olive oil

- Remove the stones from the prunes and chop the flesh into small pieces. Mix the prunes with the pork mince, sage, nutmeg and chilli powder and season well. If necessary, add a little of the beaten egg to bind together. Mould the mixture into eight patties.

- Cook the patties over a medium heat on the barbecue for about 15 minutes, turning occasionally, being careful not to let the outsides overcook before the middles are cooked right the way through.

- Season the lamb's lettuce and add a squeeze of lemon juice and the olive oil to dress the leaves. Pile the lamb's lettuce on to a large serving plate and place the patties on top.

Baked Corned Beef and Pickle Turnovers

Serves 4

I simply love corned beef hash when it's properly cooked. It makes a great winter warmer when served with plenty of potato and onion, topped with pickled red cabbage. My dad always used to have big glass sweet jars filled with pickled cabbage in the garage.

Here, I have used corned beef with bought pickle instead of cabbage – it's really tasty and is excellent for picnics.

200g (7 oz) corned beef, chilled overnight
55g (2 oz) spicy pickle
40g (1½ oz) fresh breadcrumbs
1 tsp chopped fresh thyme
1 egg, beaten
sea salt and freshly ground black pepper
beaten egg, to egg wash
8 sheets filo pastry, each measuring at least 12 × 24cm (4½ × 9½ in)

- Preheat the oven to 200°C/400°F/Gas 6 and grease a baking sheet.

- Cut the corned beef into 8mm (⅜ in) cubes and place in a bowl. Add the pickle, breadcrumbs, chopped thyme and beaten egg and season well with pepper.

- Cut out sixteen circles 12cm (4½ in) in diameter from the pastry and cover, to prevent them drying out.

- Lightly brush one pastry disc with egg wash, then cover with another pastry disc. Lightly brush egg wash over one half of the surface, top with a spoonful of the corned beef mixture, then fold over the other half of the pastry and pinch the edges to seal well. Repeat to make more turnovers.

- Brush the turnovers with egg wash and sprinkle with sea salt, then place on a baking sheet. Cook in the oven for about 15 minutes, or until golden. Remove from the oven and allow to cool.

Monkfish Kebabs with Basil and Lemon Oil

Serves 4

Many of today's 'in vogue' fish were very cheap when I first started cooking – seabass, for example, was thrown back in the sea by fishermen, and monkfish and skate were also disregarded. Some friends of mine used to have a permanent caravan in Lyme Regis and we used to water ski and generally chill out through most summer Sundays. Barbecues there were great fun – I used to buy baby dabs and monkfish from the local fishermen. Dabs can be wrapped in foil parcels with a little butter and cooked on the barbecue and monkfish can be used to make delicious kebabs. Give them a whirl and you won't be disappointed.

675g (1 lb 8 oz) skinned and boned monkfish tail fillets
bunch of fresh basil, chopped
large pinch of caster sugar
$\frac{1}{2}$ tsp Chinese five spice powder
3 tbsp olive oil
salt and freshly ground black pepper
finely grated zest and juice of 2 lemons
12 button mushrooms, brushed or wiped clean

- Cut the monkfish into 2cm (¾ in) cubes.

- Place the chopped basil in a bowl. Add the sugar, five spice powder and olive oil, mix together and season, then add the monkfish and turn to coat. Cover the bowl and allow to marinate in the fridge for 3–4 hours, or overnight if possible.

- Add the lemon juice and zest to the fish and mix again. Thread alternate pieces of monkfish and mushrooms on to skewers (don't push them too closely together) and season.

- Place the kebabs on the hot barbecue grid and cook for about 12–15 minutes, turning regularly until cooked through. Do not allow to overcook as the fish will become very tough and dry. The kebabs are perfect served with a glass of chilled Chardonnay.

Grilled Salmon Steaks with Chargrilled Limes and Spiced Braised Rice

Serves 4

Salmon is cheap these days, but when I was a little boy it was horrendously expensive. I remember my grandma carefully forking John West salmon out of a tin and mixing it with chopped onions for my grandad's sandwiches.

Salmon is a versatile fish and, because it's got a high natural fat content, it's perfect for roasting and grilling. Ask your fishmonger to cut four cutlets across the bone – I like to keep the bone in as the flesh then seems to cook much better; the skin will crisp up as well.

If the heavens open on the day of your barbecue, the salmon and lime can be cooked under a conventional grill or in a griddle pan on the hob.

225g (8 oz) basmati rice

1 tbsp vegetable oil

4 shallots, chopped

2 tsp mustard seeds

2 tsp ground turmeric

2 tsp garam masala

1 tsp allspice

1 tsp ground cumin

600ml (1 pint) boiling fish or chicken stock

3 tbsp olive oil

pinch of caster sugar

zest of 2 limes, finely grated, plus 2 whole limes

1 tsp white wine vinegar

salt and freshly ground black pepper

4 salmon cutlets, with bone and skin, about 200g (7 oz) each

3 tbsp chopped fresh coriander

Put the rice in a large bowl, pour over enough cold water to cover and leave to soak for 30 minutes. Drain well.

Heat the vegetable oil in a pan, add the shallots and spices and cook for 2–3 minutes, stirring to release all the flavours and aromas. Add the drained rice and fry for another couple of minutes, stirring continuously to coat the rice in the oil and spices. Add the stock and bring to the boil. Stir once, then cover with a tight-fitting lid and reduce the heat slightly. Allow to simmer for 10 minutes, but do not be tempted to stir the rice again during this time.

Meanwhile, mix together the olive oil, sugar, lime zest, vinegar and salt and pepper, then brush over both sides of the salmon steaks. Cut the whole limes in half.

Make sure the barbecue is hot (but not too hot), and place the salmon steaks on the grid. Season well with salt and pepper and cook for about 3–4 minutes on each side, or until just cooked through. Place the lime halves, cut side down, on to the barbecue grid at the same time, allow them to char, then turn slightly and cook for a further few minutes to make a nice pattern on the flesh; the lime juice will caramelize and taste wonderful.

Taste the rice to make sure it is just tender and has absorbed all the liquid (if it is too sticky, add just a splash of boiling water to moisten it), then add the coriander and stir to mix thoroughly. The rice can be served hot with the salmon, or allowed to cool to take on a picnic.

Serve the hot salmon on the braised rice with the limes, squeezing over the juice.

Griddled Sweetcorn with Sage Butter and Black Pepper

Serves 4

Maize was first grown in the UK in the late sixties and early seventies, and used for cattle feed during the winter months; the whole plant is mashed up and treated with preservatives to make what is known as silage. Having been brought up next door to a farm, we spent many school summer holidays charging around the neat rows of maize plants (much to the farmer's annoyance) and bringing home corn on the cobs for Dad to cook under the grill with lashings of garlic butter. This was my first real introduction to fresh vegetables – other than those grown on Dad's veg patch.

115g (4 oz) unsalted butter

4 tsp chopped fresh sage

salt and freshly ground black pepper

dash of Worcestershire sauce

4 large sweetcorn, with husk

- In a pan or using the microwave, first soften the butter, add the chopped sage and a little salt and pepper, beat well and then add a dash of Worcestershire sauce to give the dish a kick. Keep at room temperature.

- There are two ways of cooking this very simple dish. The first method is simply to barbecue the cobs directly on the grid. To do this, take off the outside green leaves and remove all the corn silk (the tassels that look like fine strands of cotton), then start to barbecue over hot coals. Because of the high sugar content of the corn, the cobs can burn easily, so once they start to colour carefully smear over a little of the butter and keep turning during the cooking so that they end up golden brown and wonderfully glazed. This will take about 15–20 minutes. Do not overcook or the corn will toughen.

- The other way to cook sweetcorn is to place each cob on a separate piece of foil, large enough to wrap around the corn to make a parcel. Smear the butter over the corn, bring the edges of the foil together and seal to enclose, then place on the barbecue. This method steams the cobs in their own juices and they don't gain any colour. Again, do not overcook.

Stir-fries

Strips of Beef with Yellow Bean Sauce and Fresh Asparagus

Serves 4

2 beef fillet tails, about 350–400g
(12–14 oz) in weight
450g (1 lb) fresh asparagus
2 tbsp vegetable oil
salt and freshly ground black pepper
4 spring onions, sliced
1 tbsp finely chopped fresh root ginger
160g jar yellow bean sauce

Fillet beef is very expensive, but the 'tails' are on average half the price, which makes this recipe an affordable treat. Only use fresh asparagus (at its best in England in late April and May) – the tinned or frozen varieties are revolting. You can use black bean sauce instead of yellow bean if you prefer.

- Cut the fillet tails into slices 1cm ($\frac{1}{2}$ in) thick then cut again into thin strips.

- Trim the asparagus. If it is young and fresh, you will need to trim only a small amount of the stalk – a good guide is to allow four times the length of the asparagus head and trim off the rest. Cut the trimmed asparagus into 2$\frac{1}{2}$cm (2 in) pieces and wash well. If the asparagus is a bit past its best, you may need to peel the end of the stalk with a potato peeler.

- Place the wok over a high heat and add half the oil. Season the beef well and add to the wok. Sauté quickly in the hot oil until it is cooked to taste. Tip the meat into a colander and keep warm. Carefully wipe out the wok using a piece of kitchen paper.

- Add the rest of the oil to the wok and heat until it just begins to smoke, then add the asparagus and season. Stir-fry for a few minutes until just tender, then add the spring onions and ginger and continue cooking for a further minute. Pour in the yellow bean sauce and warm through. Return the beef to the pan and stir to coat.

- Serve immediately with boiled rice.

Quick Ginger Chicken with Red Onions

Serves 4

Most people like to cook only the breast meat of chickens these days, presumably because it is very good, quick and easy to use. In the restaurant, we always used to have hundreds of legs left over, so I devised this tasty dish. Originally, it was for staff lunches, then it progressed on to the Brazz menu and now it's in the book.

6 chicken thighs, skinned and boned	1 tbsp Chinese oyster sauce
25g (1 oz) fresh root ginger, peeled and finely chopped	salt and freshly ground black pepper
½ tsp five spice powder	2 tbsp vegetable oil
dash of dark soy sauce	2 small red onions, thinly sliced
	2 cloves garlic, crushed

- Prepare all the ingredients to be stir-fried. Trim any excess fat off the chicken thighs then cut each one into 6–8 strips. Make sure the ginger is finely chopped – there's nothing worse than chewing on big chunks of raw ginger! Mix together the five spice powder, soy sauce and oyster sauce in a bowl and season lightly.

- Heat a wok, add half the vegetable oil and heat until smoking, then tip in the chicken and season well. Stir the chicken for 5–6 minutes, or until it has changed colour and is cooked through. Turn the chicken and its juices out of the wok on to a plate and carefully wipe the wok clean with a piece of kitchen paper.

- Add the remaining oil to the wok, then add the onions and stir-fry until just soft (if they get too dry pour in some of the juices from the chicken). Add the garlic and ginger and cook for a further 2 minutes.

- To finish the dish, return the chicken to the wok, add the soy and oyster sauce mixture and heat through. Stir well and serve with plain boiled noodles.

Mangetout with Ham, Hazelnuts and Red Chilli Oil

Some years ago I worked at Gravetye Manor, a magnificent country house hotel in West Sussex. The head chef there at that time, my friend Leigh Herbert, used to cook a wonderful dish that consisted of stir-fried mangetout, walnut oil and chicken in a puff pastry tart. Here, I've taken that idea and used ham and hazelnuts instead.

450g (1 lb) mangetout

1 red chilli

3 tbsp olive oil

55g (2 oz) toasted hazelnuts, chopped

175g (6 oz) ham slices

salt and freshly ground black pepper

- Firstly, prepare all the ingredients to be stir-fried. Top and tail the mangetout and cut any large ones in half. Cut the chilli in half lengthways and remove the seeds, then chop the flesh finely and mix into the olive oil. Place the hazelnuts in a plastic bag and crush using a rolling pin. Cut the ham into thin strips.

- Heat a wok over a medium heat, add about half the chilli oil and straightaway add the mangetout. Stir-fry for about 4 minutes, until just tender, adding a little salt to help them soften. Add the hazelnuts and ham and cook to just warm through. Season. Pile on to plates and serve with the remaining chilli oil.

- Instead of ham, you could use beef, or even smoked salmon if you're feeling flush.

Tiger Prawns with Lemon Oil and Savoy Cabbage

Serves 2

Say 'cabbage' and the word strikes fear and loathing into many people, with its associations of awful school dinners or overcooked Sunday lunches. But you should try this version – it makes a complete contrast to the horrors of old. You can also cook leeks in the same way. Both vegetables go perfectly with the tiger prawns and lemon.

> 55g (2 oz) unsalted butter
> 1 small savoy cabbage, finely shredded
> 1 small onion, thinly sliced
> salt and freshly ground black pepper
> 3 tbsp olive oil
> 175g (6 oz) raw, shelled tiger prawns
> finely grated zest and juice of ½ lemon

● Heat the butter in a wok until it is just bubbling, add the cabbage and onion, season well and stir over a medium heat until the cabbage wilts. Do not overcook. Carefully spoon the cabbage out of the wok and place in a colander to drain.

● Using a piece of kitchen paper, carefully wipe out the wok and place it back on the hob. Turn up the heat, add the olive oil and when it starts to smoke add the tiger prawns. Season with salt and pepper. Cook over a high heat until the prawns begin to turn pink, then add the lemon zest and cook for a further minute. Add the lemon juice and the drained cabbage. Warm through, making sure that the prawns do not overcook. Season again if necessary and serve straightaway.

Stir-fried New Potatoes with Chilli, Tomatoes and Basil

Serves 2, or 4 as an accompaniment

I first cooked this dish on *Ready Steady Cook*, so I know it cooks in 20 minutes! The potatoes cook so quickly in their own steam that they retain all their vitamins and flavour. Sometimes spicy stir-fries such as this one are better cooked quickly and then reheated slowly the next day when the flavour is different again.

450g (1 lb) small Charlotte new potatoes
½ tsp cumin seeds
2 tbsp vegetable oil
1 red chilli, seeded and chopped
1 clove garlic, crushed
4 ripe plum tomatoes, seeded and roughly chopped
2 tbsp roughly chopped fresh basil
salt and freshly ground black pepper

- Cut the potatoes in half lengthways.

- Heat a frying pan, add the cumin seeds and dry-fry over a low heat for a couple of minutes, stirring all the time until they brown. Do not allow the cumin to burn. (Cooking spices in this way really brings out their flavour and aroma.)

- Heat the vegetable oil in a wok or large sauté pan until just smoking, then reduce the heat, add the chilli, garlic and toasted cumin seeds and cook for 2–3 minutes until they take on a little colour. Again, do not allow to burn. Add the potatoes, stir well, season and turn down the heat to medium. Cover the wok or pan with a lid, if you have one, or use a piece of foil and cover tightly. Cook for about 20 minutes, or until the potatoes are tender, turning occasionally.

- When the potatoes are cooked, add the chopped tomatoes and basil and continue cooking for a few minutes until the tomatoes start to break down. Season and serve straightaway.

Cauliflower with Turmeric, Caraway and Green Beans

Serves 4

I once worked for about six weeks with some Indian chefs. It was an amazing experience: six or eight chefs looked after and cooked for the main man and his manservant, and another chef and his wife (who came from Wimbledon) cooked for the chefs, if you see what I mean. Then there was me, making luscious puddings for everyone. Kumar, the cooks' cook, taught me how to prepare real Indian food and opened my eyes to the best vegetarian cuisine in the world.

6 tbsp olive oil

1 tsp caraway seeds

1 tsp turmeric

1 large cauliflower, cut into florets

225g (8 oz) fine green beans, cut into 2½cm (1 in) pieces

finely grated zest of ½ lemon

1 tbsp chopped fresh coriander

salt and freshly ground black pepper

- Heat the oil in a wok over a moderate heat. Add the caraway seeds and turmeric and cook for 1–2 minutes to roast the spices, but don't allow them to burn.

- Add the cauliflower to the wok and stir to coat with the spices, then add the beans and toss together. Add the lemon zest and 4 teaspoons of water, then season and cover with a lid (if your wok does not have a lid, you can use a piece of foil). Cook for 20–25 minutes, stirring occasionally, until the cauliflower is tender. Finally, add the coriander and check the seasoning. This is a great accompaniment for grilled chicken or pork chops.

Pasta and Rice

Marinated Pasta Ribbons
Serves 4

I love eating pasta. This dish is packed full of flavour and can be eaten on its own, or you can serve it with fish, chicken or roasted Mediterranean vegetables – a perfect meal for summer.

3 tbsp olive oil

1 tsp balsamic vinegar

1 tsp wholegrain mustard

2 tsp chopped fresh basil

2 tsp chopped fresh oregano

2 tsp chopped fresh chervil

2 tsp chopped fresh tarragon

1 clove garlic, crushed

8 cherry tomatoes, cut into quarters

500g (1 lb 2 oz) fresh fettuccine

salt and freshly ground black pepper

● Mix together the olive oil, vinegar and mustard in a large bowl, then add the herbs and garlic and stir well. Finally, stir in the cherry tomatoes and allow to stand for 1 hour.

● Meanwhile, cook the fettuccine in a large pan with plenty of boiling water for 3 minutes, or until just tender. Drain the pasta through a colander then refresh under cold running water to stop it sticking together. Drain well again.

● Add the pasta to the dressing and toss together to coat. Season and allow to stand at room temperature for 1–2 hours to allow the flavours to infuse.

● Eat cold, or just warmed through under a preheated grill for a few seconds.

Penne with Five Cheeses

I know this seems like a bit of overkill on the cheese front but don't be put off by it. The secret to this dish is to let the cheese just start to melt so you can still see the cubes.

450g (1 lb) dried penne pasta

75g (2¾ oz) Gorgonzola

75g (2¾ oz) Cheddar

75g (2¾ oz) Red Leicester

75g (2¾ oz) Pecorino

2 tbsp olive oil

1 small onion, finely chopped

200ml (7 fl oz) white wine

500ml (18 fl oz) double cream

salt and freshly ground black pepper

25g (1 oz) Parmesan, grated

2 tbsp chopped fresh marjoram

- Cook the pasta according to the packet instructions, then drain well.

- Cut the Gorgonzola, Cheddar, Red Leicester and Pecorino cheeses into small cubes.

- Heat the oil in a large pan, then add the onion and cook gently until softened. Do not allow to brown. Add the wine and simmer rapidly to reduce by about half.

- Stir the cream into the reduced wine and bring to the boil, then season to taste. Add the cubed cheese, grated Parmesan, marjoram and drained pasta and stir over a gentle heat until the cheeses just begin to melt and coat the pasta. Pile on to plates.

Farfalle Salmon

Serves 4

This is a great way of having smoked salmon at half the price – you can buy packets of trimmings which are a lot cheaper than the usual slices. The sharp lemon edge is a nice touch, but take care not to overkill the salmon.

300g (10½ oz) dried farfalle pasta
15g (½ oz) butter
2 large shallots, finely chopped
finely grated zest and juice of 1 lemon
200ml (7 fl oz) white wine
500ml (18 fl oz) double cream
salt and freshly ground black pepper
about ½ tsp caster sugar
2 tbsp chopped fresh tarragon
75g (2½ oz) Parmesan, freshly grated
150g (5½ oz) smoked salmon, cut into thin strips

- Cook the pasta according to the packet instructions, then drain well.

- Heat the butter in a large pan, then add the shallots and cook gently until softened. Do not allow to brown. Add the lemon zest to the pan and cook, stirring, for a further 2 minutes. Pour the wine into the pan, increase the heat and bring to the boil, then simmer rapidly until the wine has reduced by about half.

- Add the cream to the reduced wine and bring to a simmer. Stir in the lemon juice and season, then add sugar to taste.

- Stir the drained pasta into the sauce with the tarragon, Parmesan and salmon and gently warm through. Spoon on to plates and serve.

Pasta Shells with Petits Pois, Horseradish and Roast Beef Leftovers

Serves 4

This is a classic example of a chef going home at midnight, having a very large gin and tonic, then thinking to himself, 'Hmm, I'm a bit peckish,' opening the fridge and cupboards and using up whatever has been left hanging around. But, believe me, the results are delicious.

300g (10½ oz) dried pasta shells

280g (10 oz) frozen petits pois

4 thick slices cold, rare roast beef, cut into 1cm (½ in) slices

4 tsp creamed horseradish

2–3 tbsp olive oil

salt and freshly ground black pepper

- Cook the pasta according to the packet instructions.

- Meanwhile, cook the petits pois in a pan of boiling salted water for about 2–3 minutes, or until tender.

- Drain the pasta into a colander then return to the pan. Drain the peas through a sieve and add to the pasta, together with the beef, then add the horseradish and olive oil, season and pile on to plates.

Quick and Easy Tomato Sauce

Serves 4

This is incredibly quick and easy. You can serve it as it is with the pasta of your choice, or you can use it as a base for other pasta sauce recipes, such as the ones on pages 56 and 57.

400g can chopped tomatoes
1½ tsp salt
1½ tsp freshly ground black pepper
1 clove garlic, crushed
1 small onion, finely chopped
2 tsp caster sugar
2 tsp white wine vinegar
2 tsp tomato purée
3 tbsp olive oil
2 tsp fresh thyme leaves

- Place all the ingredients in a pan, together with 200ml (7 fl oz) of water, bring to the boil, then reduce the heat and simmer for 10 minutes.

- You can leave this sauce chunky or, if you prefer, tip it into a food processor and blitz until smooth. Check the seasoning before serving.

Spaghetti with Tomato Sauce and Tuna

Serves 4

I really enjoy tinned tuna fish. Frankly, it's awful on its own but when it's put together with other well-chosen ingredients it can be delicious. This is a simple after-work supper which never fails to hit the spot.

400g (14 oz) dried spaghetti

2 tbsp olive oil

2 shallots, finely chopped

1 small red chilli, seeds removed and finely chopped

200ml (7 fl oz) white wine

1 quantity *Quick and easy tomato sauce*, see page 55

500ml (18 fl oz) double cream

285g can tuna chunks, drained

2 tbsp chopped fresh parsley

25g (1 oz) Parmesan, grated

salt and freshly ground black pepper

- Cook the pasta according to the packet instructions, then drain.

- Heat the oil in a large pan then add the shallots and chilli and cook gently until softened. Do not allow to brown. Add the wine and simmer rapidly until reduced by about three-quarters.

- Stir in the tomato sauce, cream and tuna (try not to break up the tuna too much) and bring back to the boil, then stir in the drained pasta, parsley and Parmesan and toss to coat. Season and spoon on to plates.

Chicken Rigatoni

Serves 4

The combination of chicken, basil and garlic is a match made in heaven, though you could use turkey or even guinea fowl instead of the chicken if you prefer. This is a wonderfully quick dish to prepare.

250g (9 oz) dried rigatoni pasta

2 tbsp olive oil

3 chicken breast fillets, skin removed and cut into bite-sized pieces

1 clove garlic, crushed

300ml ($\frac{1}{2}$ pint) white wine

150ml ($\frac{1}{4}$ pint) double cream

1 quantity *Quick and easy tomato sauce*, see page 55

1–2 tbsp chopped fresh basil

55g (2 oz) Parmesan cheese, freshly grated

salt and freshly ground black pepper

- Cook the pasta according to the packet instructions, then drain.

- Heat the oil in a large pan. Add the chicken and garlic and stir over a fairly high heat until the chicken is golden brown all over. Add the wine to the pan, bring to the boil and simmer rapidly until reduced by about half. Stir in the cream and tomato sauce, bring to a simmer, then cook for about 5 minutes, or until the chicken is cooked through.

- Add the drained pasta to the sauce with the basil and Parmesan and add seasoning to taste. Stir to coat and warm through. Spoon on to plates and serve.

Saffron Pilaff with Crispy Bacon and Basil

Serves 4

Saffron rice cooked this way is both tasty and quick. The addition of the bacon in this recipe was inspired by a late-night foray to the fridge, and it works very well. This rice makes a good partner to roast chicken or lamb chops.

55g (2 oz) unsalted butter
1 small onion, finely chopped
2 pinches saffron strands
225g (8 oz) long grain rice
600ml (1 pint) hot chicken stock
8 rashers smoked back bacon
salt and freshly ground black pepper
2 tbsp chopped fresh basil

 Preheat the oven to 190°C/375°F/Gas 5 and preheat the grill to high.

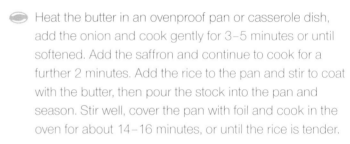 Heat the butter in an ovenproof pan or casserole dish, add the onion and cook gently for 3–5 minutes or until softened. Add the saffron and continue to cook for a further 2 minutes. Add the rice to the pan and stir to coat with the butter, then pour the stock into the pan and season. Stir well, cover the pan with foil and cook in the oven for about 14–16 minutes, or until the rice is tender.

Meanwhile, cook the bacon under the grill until golden and crispy.

Remove the cooked rice from the oven, take off the foil lid and stir well. Add a little extra butter if it is too sticky. Season, then stir in the basil and allow to stand for 2–3 minutes so that the flavours infuse.

Pile the pilaff on to plates and top with the crispy bacon.

Curries

Spiced Lamb Stew with Fruits

Serves 4

I first came across the idea of adding dried fruits and spices to meat and fish when I worked in the Lake District. Whitehaven had been a major spice port in years gone by and the area's exotic connections can still be traced in traditional Lakeland fare like Cumberland sausages, Cumberland Rum Nicky and the world-famous Grasmere Gingerbread. I put all the spices I can find into this delicious stew. I know it probably looks like a drag to get them all together but persevere and it's well worth it. It should be served not too hot, accompanied by a large bowl of mash.

675g (1½ lb) lean shoulder of lamb, diced
½ tsp chilli powder
2 tsp black mustard seeds
½ tsp ground allspice
1 tsp ground cinnamon
1 tsp garam masala
1 tsp ground cloves
1 tsp ground black pepper
1 tsp ground nutmeg
125ml (4 fl oz) olive oil
2 onions, peeled and sliced
3 tbsp plain flour
1 tbsp tomato purée
2 cloves garlic, crushed
1 beef stock cube
400ml (14 fl oz) fresh orange juice
salt and freshly ground
black pepper, to season
about 4 tsp caster sugar
225g (8 oz) dried prunes, stones in
225g (8 oz) dried apricots
mashed potato, to serve

- Place the lamb in a large bowl, sprinkle over all the dried spices and toss to coat. Cover the dish with clingfilm and marinate overnight in the fridge.

- Preheat the oven to 160°C/325°F/Gas 3. Heat half the oil in a heavy-based casserole dish until smoking, add the onions and cook until softened and slightly browned. Remove the onions from the casserole and add the lamb to the pan, together with the remaining oil and all the spices. Cook quickly to brown all over, then stir in the flour and tomato purée. Add the garlic, stock cube, orange juice and 500ml (18 fl oz) of water and stir until simmering, making sure the mixture doesn't catch and burn on the bottom. Season well with salt and pepper and add sugar to taste. Finally, add the dried fruits.

- Cover the casserole with a tight-fitting lid, and cook in the oven for about 2 hours, or until the lamb is tender, stirring occasionally. Serve straight from the pot with mashed potato.

Ben's Curry

Serves 4

You wouldn't believe the trouble I had trying to get hold of this recipe. Ben, who created it, worked for me last year and used to cook this dish for the staff. He went off to cook in a French ski chalet for a season, and trying to prise the recipe out of him has taken a lot of time and perseverance. But the curry is delicious and well worth the effort of tracking it down.

2 tbsp vegetable oil

900g (2 lb) boneless, rolled shoulder of lamb, trimmed and cut into 3cm (1¼ in) cubes

2 onions, roughly chopped

4 cloves garlic, crushed

1 tbsp grated fresh ginger

1 tbsp plain flour

1 tbsp ground turmeric

1 tbsp garam masala

1 tbsp ground cumin

1 tsp chilli powder

6–8 large tomatoes, chopped

1 chicken stock cube, made up into stock as per packet instructions

400g can coconut milk

250g (9 oz) baby spinach leaves, stalks removed

200g (7 oz) sheep's yoghurt

salt and freshly ground black pepper

Heat 1 tablespoon of the oil in a large pan, add the lamb and cook over a high heat to brown it quickly all over. Remove the lamb from the pan and place in a colander to drain. Add the remaining oil to the pan, together with the onions, garlic and ginger, and cook gently for a few minutes until softened and golden brown. Add the flour and spices and cook for a few more minutes.

Add the tomatoes and coconut milk and return the lamb to the pan. Add just enough of the made-up stock to cover the meat, and stir to release all the bits from the bottom of the pan. Then simmer very gently for about 1½ hours, until the lamb is tender, stirring occasionally.

Skim any excess fat off the surface. Stir in the spinach and cook for a few minutes until just wilted, then stir in the yoghurt and season. Serve with rice.

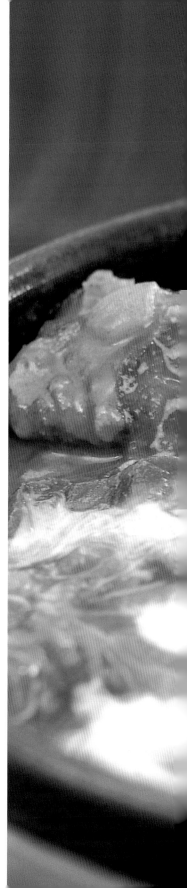

Kumar's Curried Vegetables

Serves 4

This recipe came from a young Indian chef I once worked with (see page 48) whose food was very simple and very tasty. This vegetable curry is delicious and subtle without being too hot and spicy. You can use it as a base for any combination of vegetables and potatoes you wish to include.

2 tbsp vegetable oil

1 tbsp finely grated root ginger

2 bay leaves

4 whole cloves

$\frac{1}{2}$ tsp ground cinnamon

$\frac{1}{2}$ tsp ground coriander

$\frac{1}{2}$ tsp ground cumin

$\frac{1}{2}$ tsp ground turmeric

115g (4 oz) ground almonds

6 large plum tomatoes, seeded and roughly chopped

salt and freshly ground pepper

2 tbsp double cream

300g (10$\frac{1}{2}$ oz) baby carrots, scraped, topped and tailed and cut in half lengthways

1 cauliflower, cut into small florets

175g (6 oz) fine green beans, topped and tailed and cut in half

- Heat the oil in a large pan, add the ginger and all the spices and fry for 2–3 minutes until they are browned, but not burnt. Add the almonds and tomatoes and cook over a medium heat for a further 7–8 minutes, until the tomatoes begin to break down. Season well, then add the cream.

- Parcook the vegetables in boiling salted water for 5 minutes, then drain well. Add the drained vegetables to the sauce, cover with a lid and cook gently for about 20 minutes, or until the vegetables are tender, stirring occasionally.

Gerry's Chicken Curry

Serves 4–6

We used to have a pub that adjoined the Castle Hotel called Minstrels. Gerry was the chef there for years and he developed this curry. It's not exactly authentic, but it's very tasty. He now works in the main kitchen with me, and whenever he cooks it for the staff we all devour it.

4 tbsp vegetable oil

4 skinless, boneless chicken breasts, about 140g (5 oz) each, cut into strips 1cm (½ in) wide

1 large onion, chopped

2 carrots, peeled and cut into 1cm (½ in) cubes

2 sticks celery, cut into 1cm (½ in) cubes

1 red and 1 green pepper, seeds removed and diced

2 cloves garlic, crushed

2 Granny Smith apples, cored and cut into 1cm (½ in) cubes, skins left on

3–4 tbsp mild Madras curry powder

55g (2 oz) plain flour

2 chicken stock cubes

1 tbsp tomato purée

salt and freshly ground black pepper

2 tbsp unsweetened desiccated coconut

2–3 tbsp mango chutney

- Heat the oil in a large pan, add the chicken and cook quickly until browned, then add the vegetables, garlic and apples and cook for 3–4 minutes, stirring occasionally. Add the curry powder and stir to coat, then add the flour, stock cubes and tomato purée and mix well.

- Gradually stir in about 850ml (1 ½ pints) of boiling water, a little at a time, then season and bring to the boil. Reduce the heat and simmer gently for 15 minutes, stirring occasionally.

- Add the coconut and mango chutney to taste, and cook for a further 15 minutes, or until the chicken is cooked through.

- Season again if necessary and serve with boiled rice and poppadums.

Green Fish Curry with Coconut Milk

Serves 4

I find Thai food lighter and tastier than Chinese, and more subtle than Indian food. Serve this dish with boiled basmati rice for a perfect summer lunch or dinner. You can add more or less curry paste, depending on how hot you like your curry.

200ml (7 fl oz) coconut milk

4 small shallots, finely chopped

1 tsp caster sugar

2 level tsp green Thai curry paste

1 tsp tamarind paste

salt and freshly ground black pepper

4 pieces cod, pollack or salmon fillet,
about 140–175g (5–6 oz) each

1 tbsp chopped fresh coriander

⬤ Pour the coconut milk into a large pan (it should be wide enough to lay the fish pieces side by side), add the shallots, sugar, curry paste and tamarind paste, season well and bring to the boil. Place the fish in a single layer in the pan, cover and simmer gently for about 10–15 minutes, until the fish is just very slightly undercooked – it will finish cooking while it is standing before you serve it.

⬤ Carefully transfer the fish to deep bowls, spoon the sauce over the top and sprinkle on the coriander.

Fish

Fish Cakes

Serves 4

I remember having awful frozen fish cakes when I was a kid. But once I decided to cook them myself and put them together in my own way, I found they tasted really good. They are also very simple to make. I've used salmon and cod here, but most soft-fleshed fish make good cakes. The secret is not to boil the fish when you cook it at the start, just simmer it and leave it slightly undercooked. Other tips are to season the fish cake mixture well and add a dash of olive oil to keep it moist.

- Cook the potatoes in a pan of boiling water until tender, then drain. In another pan, poach the fish in gently simmering water for about 10–15 minutes, or until it just begins to flake. When I poach fish I like to add 2 tablespoons of white wine vinegar and ½ teaspoon of salt to every 600ml (1 pint) of water in the pan.

- Heat the butter in a small pan, add the onions and cook gently until softened, but do not allow to brown.

- Mash the potatoes, flake the fish and mix together with the onion and herbs in a large bowl, then season. Mould the mixture into small balls about the size of an apricot, and, using a small amount of olive oil to moisten the mixture, flatten slightly to make patties. Dust the fish cakes in flour, dip them in the eggs and coat in the breadcrumbs. Chill in the fridge for at least 1 hour.

- Heat the vegetable oil in a frying pan, add the fish cakes and shallow-fry until golden brown and heated through, turning regularly. Drain on kitchen paper. Serve with tartar sauce and salad.

225g (8 oz) potatoes
225g (8 oz) salmon fillet, skinned
225g (8 oz) cod fillet, skinned
55g (2 oz) butter
2 onions, finely chopped
115g (4 oz) chopped mixed fresh herbs –
basil, parsley and tarragon
salt and freshly ground black pepper
dash of olive oil
115g (4 oz) plain flour
3 eggs, beaten
about 450g (1 lb) breadcrumbs
vegetable oil, for shallow-frying

Fish, Chips and Mushy Peas

Serves 4

This is my favourite meal of all time. You can't beat fish and chips if you do them properly. I was virtually brought up on real Lancashire fish and chips, spending every summer holiday in Blackpool. My mum still does real hand-cut crinkle chips which are the best ever. Do keep the skin on the fish – in my opinion it's the best bit.

225g (8 oz) dried marrowfat peas

$\frac{1}{2}$ tsp bicarbonate of soda

salt

4–6 large potatoes, Maris Piper, white King Edward or Bintje, peeled

vegetable oil, for deep-frying

4 fish fillets, cod, haddock or huss, about 225g (8 oz) each

1 quantity batter, see page 130

- Place the peas in a large container then pour over double their volume of water. Stir in a pinch of bicarb and allow to stand overnight.

- Wash the peas well under cold water and drain. Place in a pan and cover with cold water. Add a couple of pinches of salt and $\frac{1}{2}$ teaspoon of bicarb (to help them cook evenly and keep their colour). Bring to the boil, then simmer and cook until the peas are broken down and mushy – this can take anywhere between 40 minutes and 3 hours, depending on the peas and how long you have soaked them. You may need to top up the pan with a little extra water to make sure that they don't burn and stick to the bottom of the pan.

- Cut the potatoes into thin slices then into thin chips. Wash the chips well, then drain on a clean tea-towel.

- The secret of cooking good chips is to fry them twice. First heat the oil to 150–170°C (300°–350°F) and 'blanch' the chips. At this stage, you are cooking them until they are soft but have no colour. Remove them from the oil and leave to cool. Increase the heat of the oil to 185°C (370°F).

- Season the fish well, then drop in the batter and coat evenly. Deep-fry in the preheated oil until the batter is crisp and golden, turning the fish over every few minutes. (You may need to cook them a couple at a time, to avoid cramming the fryer). Remove the fish from the oil and keep warm, but do not cover – this batter stays crisp for a good while.

- Return the chips to the oil and fry until crisp and golden (new oil will not colour the chips very much so don't worry if they don't brown the first couple of times you use the oil, it's more important that they are crisp). Drain on kitchen paper and sprinkle with salt.

- Serve with tartar sauce and bread and butter.

Roast Cod and Bacon

Serves 4

Twenty years ago, cod was one of the cheaper fishes and, being a good Catholic family, we always had fish on Fridays. I used to fish for cod as a kid off Folkestone Pier in the winter months, and can still recall the sheer excitement of watching such a large fish being reeled in. The humble cod is great in so many guises – it can be fried, baked, stewed, roasted, poached or even served raw like sushi. In this dish I keep the skin on the fish, partly to help hold it together, but also because the skin tastes delicious when crispy.

115g (4 oz) unsalted butter

375g (13 oz) baby plum tomatoes, chilled

salt and freshly ground black pepper

8 rashers smoked back bacon, rinds removed

4 thick pieces cod fillet, skin on and pin bones removed, about 225g (8 oz) each

450g (1 lb) mashed potato, see page 116

25g (1 oz) pitted black olives, roughly chopped

½ lemon

Preheat oven to 230°C/450°F/Gas 8 and preheat the grill to high.

In a large ovenproof frying pan, gently heat the butter until melted. Place the tomatoes in a shallow ovenproof dish and brush over a little of the melted butter (as the tomatoes have just come out of the fridge, the butter should set slightly), then season.

Grill the bacon on both sides until crisp.

Increase the heat under the frying pan and cook until the butter just begins to foam and turn golden brown. Season the cod fillets well (cod can take quite a lot of salt and pepper), then place the fish, skin side down, in the foaming butter. Cook for about 3–4 minutes, then transfer the pan to the oven and cook for a further 5–6 minutes, or until fish is just cooked. (If you do not have an ovenproof frying pan, you can start the fish off in a frying pan then gently lift the cod into a baking dish, pour over the butter and place in the oven.) You can tell if 'flaky' fish is cooked by gently pressing the flesh – there should be a slight springy resistance to the touch. If the fish is overcooked the larger flakes will flake almost at the touch.

Reduce the grill temperature and grill the tomatoes under a medium heat until just tender.

To serve, fold the olives into the mashed potatoes, then spoon some into the middle of the plates. Carefully add a piece of fish, skin side up, and top each with two rashers of crispy bacon. Scatter the tomatoes around the edge of the plate. Warm the buttery juices from the cooking pan, add just a squeeze of lemon juice, then spoon over the top.

Grilled Mackerel with Tasty Tomato Sauce

Serves 4

One of my favourite summer fish, mackerel is nutritious, flavoursome and rich in vitamin D. It works well with gooseberries and rhubarb, and it also takes most spices in its stride. But the best way to cook it, I think, is as simply as possible – preferably flashed under a grill or barbecue.

Mackerel deteriorates quickly, so use it soon after purchase. If you are very keen, and can get to Lyme Regis in the summer, the mackerel boats make a great afternoon outing.

2 tbsp olive oil

1 onion, finely chopped

2 cloves garlic, finely chopped

400g can chopped tomatoes

2 tsp chopped fresh basil

2 tsp chopped fresh tarragon

1 tsp caster sugar

1 tsp malt vinegar

2 tsp tomato purée

salt and freshly ground black pepper

4 very fresh, large mackerel fillets, about 225–280g (8–10 oz) each

25g (1 oz) butter, melted

- Warm the olive oil in a pan, add the onion and garlic and cook for 3–4 minutes, until softened and golden brown. Add the tomatoes, basil, tarragon, sugar, vinegar and tomato purée and season well. Simmer gently for about 30 minutes, or until the sauce is thick. Check the seasoning and add a little more salt, pepper and sugar if necessary – you may also need to add a little more olive oil to moisten the sauce, although it should not be too sloppy. Keep the sauce warm on the hob, but do not allow to boil.

- Preheat the grill to high. Place the mackerel, skin side up, on a non-stick baking sheet and season. Spoon over the melted butter and place under the grill. Grill the skin side only until the skin blisters and bubbles. Do not overcook.

- To serve, spoon the tomato compote on to plates and top with the mackerel fillets. Serve with crusty bread and a large bowl of salad.

Spicy Sprats with Yoghurt and Mint

Serves 4

Sprats are my dad's favourite tea-time special – he will quite happily devour dozens of them. He prefers plain lemon juice with his sprats, but they taste wonderful with this yoghurt dressing.

300g (10½ oz) natural yoghurt

1 tbsp chopped fresh mint

1–2 tsp caster sugar

85g (3 oz) plain flour

½ tsp garam masala

½ tsp ground cumin

1 tsp chilli powder

salt and freshly ground black pepper

550g (1 lb 4 oz) large sprats (as large as possible)

4 tbsp vegetable oil

- Mix together the yoghurt, mint and sugar to taste and allow to stand for 2 hours.

- Place the flour, spices, a twist of pepper and a pinch of salt in a large plastic bag. Pat the sprats dry using kitchen paper then add to the bag. Pinch the open edges of the bags together and shake to coat the fish.

- Heat half the vegetable oil in a large non-stick frying pan. Remove the sprats from the bag and shake off any excess flour, then add to the hot oil (you will probably need to cook them in two batches). Fry over a medium heat for 2–3 minutes on each side, then transfer to a plate and allow to rest for another couple of minutes.

- Now for the best bit (make sure you have plenty of kitchen paper at the ready). Pile the sprats on to a big plate and help yourself. Take the warm sprats between thumb and forefinger, pinch off the tail then firmly pinch the head and spine together just below the gills and pull so that the whole bone pulls out. Dip the sprats in the yoghurt dressing and eat. Serve with a green salad.

Seared Salmon with Roasted Spices and Spring Onion Crème Fraîche

Serves 4

This is a 'cheffy' recipe and more complex than some, although it is still fairly straightforward. It's one of my all-time favourites and both looks and tastes wonderful. It always sells very well at the Castle so I had to include it here. Salmon's good value for money at the moment too.

For the roasted spices:

2 tbsp coriander seeds

1 tbsp cumin seeds

3 tbsp black peppercorns

1 tsp green cardamom pods

2 tsp ground cinnamon

2 tsp whole cloves

2 tsp freshly grated nutmeg

2 tsp mustard seeds

bunch of spring onions, finely chopped

3 tbsp white wine vinegar

1 tbsp chopped fresh chives

300ml (½ pint) crème fraîche

salt and freshly ground black pepper

pinch of caster sugar

115g (4 oz) couscous

225ml (8 fl oz) boiling fish stock

1 red pepper, seeded and finely chopped

3 tbsp olive oil

4 pieces salmon fillet with skin, about 115g (4 oz) each, all bones removed

3 tbsp vegetable oil

few sprigs of watercress

- Heat a frying pan, add the spices and cook for 1–2 minutes to 'roast' them, stirring to make sure they do not burn. Tip the spices on to a chopping board and crush by pressing down heavily on them using a heavy-based pan. Alternatively, place them in a thick plastic bag and beat with a rolling pin.

- Mix the spring onions, vinegar and chives into the crème fraîche, season and add a little sugar to taste.

- Place the couscous in a heatproof bowl, pour over the boiling fish stock then cover with clingfilm. Allow to stand for 10 minutes – the couscous will absorb all the liquid.

- Stir the couscous well, add the chopped pepper and olive oil, stir again and season.

- Sprinkle the spice mixture generously over the salmon and season with salt. Heat the vegetable oil in a non-stick frying pan until the oil just begins to smoke, then add the salmon, spice side down. Reduce the heat slightly and cook for a few minutes, until a white liquid starts to run out from the fish – the top will still be raw, but should be warm. Remove the pan from the heat and allow to stand in a warm place for about 10 minutes, or until the fish has cooked through – the flesh should flake when pressed gently.

- Pile the couscous on to plates and add the watercress. Sit the salmon, crust side upwards, on top and spoon over some of the crème fraîche mixture. Serve immediately.

Warm Salmon with Eggs and Real Sautéed Potatoes

Serves 4

When I worked in the Lakes one of my good mates, Des, used to love ham and sautéed potatoes and he'd spend a lot of time cooking the potatoes just right. Here are his 'real' sautéed potatoes – the only way to cook them.

8 medium-sized potatoes, skins on

3 tsp salt

1 onion, peeled and cut into quarters

1 carrot, peeled and cut into large chunks

1 tsp black peppercorns

1 stick celery, cut into large chunks

150–175ml (5–6 fl oz) white wine vinegar

salt and freshly ground black pepper

1 tbsp vegetable oil

25g (1 oz) unsalted butter

4 pieces skinless salmon fillet, about 125g (4½ oz) each

4–8 eggs

- Place the potatoes in a large pan and pour on enough cold water to cover. Add 1 teaspoon of salt and bring to the boil, then reduce the heat and simmer for about 20–25 minutes, or until the potatoes are tender (you should be able to push a sharp knife through them without any resistance). Strain off the liquid and allow to cool.

- Meanwhile, make the stock: place the onion, carrot, peppercorns, celery, 100ml (3½ fl oz) of vinegar and 2 teaspoons of salt in a pan, together with 1.2 litres (2 pints) of water, and bring to the boil. Reduce the heat and simmer for about 35 minutes.

- Peel the cooled potatoes carefully, cut into slices 2cm (¾ in) thick and season well with salt and pepper.

- Heat the oil in a large frying pan, add the butter and continue cooking until it begins to foam, then add the potatoes (you may need to cook them in two batches). Cook over a medium heat until they are nice and brown and crispy on both sides. Keep warm.

While the potatoes are cooking, strain the stock into a large measuring jug. Top up the liquid with enough boiling water to make it back up to 1.2 litres (2 pints), then pour the liquid into a pan and bring to the boil. Add the salmon to the pan and quickly bring to the boil, then remove the pan from the heat. Cover with a lid and allow to stand for 12–15 minutes, or until the fish is cooked.

To make the poached eggs, half-fill a medium-sized pan with cold water and add 50–75ml (2–2½ fl oz) of vinegar or lemon juice (I also add a pinch of salt to the water as I think it helps to coagulate the egg white). Bring the pan to the boil and, when the water is bubbling, crack in the eggs. Bring the water back to simmering point, then reduce the heat and simmer gently for 2–3 minutes, or until the eggs are just set and still a little soft. Again, you may need to do this in two batches. Carefully remove from the water using a slotted spoon and drain on kitchen paper.

Pile the sautéed potatoes on to plates and add an egg and a piece of salmon to each. You can serve this with a little mayonnaise if you want to.

Flash-fried Smoked Salmon with Green Beans and Chive Dressing

Serves 4

Smoked salmon is a bit pricy, but it makes a delicious treat and it can actually go a long way, as you will see in this recipe. This dish is quick and simple to prepare and tastes wonderful. Serve it as a summer starter or, in larger portions, as a main course.

450g (1 lb) fine green beans, topped and tailed

1 tsp Dijon mustard

pinch of caster sugar

salt and freshly ground black pepper

4 tsp white wine vinegar

4 tsp vegetable oil

4 tsp olive oil, plus a little extra for frying

2 tbsp chopped fresh chives

225g (8 oz) sliced smoked salmon

- Cook the beans in a pan of boiling salted water for 2–3 minutes, or until just cooked (you don't want them too crunchy). Drain and refresh under cold running water so that they keep their brilliant green colour. Drain well again.

- In a large bowl, mix together the mustard and sugar, then season. Stir in the vinegar then, with an electric or balloon whisk, gradually whisk the vegetable oil and olive oil in a thin stream, until they are fully incorporated. Adjust the seasoning if necessary, then add the beans and chives and stir well. Allow to stand for 1 hour at room temperature.

- Heat a dash of olive oil in a non-stick frying pan until the oil just begins to smoke. Add the slices of salmon, one at a time, and flash-fry for 2–3 seconds on one side then lift out. Do not overcook – the uncooked side must stay undercooked.

- Pile the beans on to plates and top with the salmon. Serve with boiled new potatoes.

Prawn, Chilli and Coriander Mayo with Melba Toast

Serves 4

I love prawns in any shape or form. This recipe is a modern version of that old British classic, the prawn cocktail. The only things to serve with it are Melba toast or buttered brown bread, and possibly a squeeze of lemon.

300ml (½ pint) mayonnaise
2 red chillies, seeded and chopped
1 small onion, finely chopped
2 tsp finely chopped fresh ginger
2 tbsp chopped fresh chives
2 tbsp chopped fresh coriander
2 tbsp Heinz tomato ketchup
dash of Worcestershire sauce
250g (9 oz) peeled cooked prawns
salt and freshly ground black pepper
½ lemon
6 medium slices white bread

- Preheat the grill. In a large bowl, mix together the mayonnaise, chilli, onion, ginger, chives, coriander, tomato ketchup and Worcestershire sauce. Add the prawns and mix together, then season with salt and pepper and a little lemon juice to taste. If possible, leave to marinate in the fridge for 2–3 hours.

- Toast both sides of the bread under the grill until golden brown. Cut off the crusts then, using a bread knife, cut horizontally through each slice of toast to give two thin pieces. Cool slightly, then rub the uncooked sides of the toast together to remove any loose crumbs. Cut each slice in half diagonally, reduce the heat of the grill, then toast the uncooked sides of the bread until golden, crispy and crunchy.

- Serve the prawn mayonnaise in a bowl and arrange the toast around the edge.

Meat

Slow-roasted Chicken Thighs and Bacon with Onion Stew

Serves 4

I'm a leg rather than a breast man – when it comes to cooking chicken. Thighs suit slow-roasting and braising perfectly and they seem to stay juicy and succulent even if you accidentally leave them in the oven for a few minutes longer than you should. Also they are about half the price of breasts. Chicken cooked this way is perfect eaten cold on picnics accompanied by new potatoes.

8 rashers back bacon – maple cure, if you can find it
8 chicken thighs
2 tbsp vegetable oil
salt and freshly ground black pepper
4 large onions, sliced
250ml (9 fl oz) dry white wine
1 tsp caster sugar
1 tbsp chopped fresh basil
850ml (1½ pints) fresh chicken stock

- Preheat the oven to 160°C/325°F/Gas 3. Wrap a bacon rasher around each chicken thigh and place on a non-stick baking sheet. Drizzle a little oil over each piece of chicken and season well. Roast slowly in the oven for about 1–1¼ hours, or until the chicken is cooked through.

- Meanwhile, place the onions in a pan with the wine, sugar, basil and chicken stock. Bring to the boil, then simmer rapidly to reduce the liquid until it is thick and syrupy – you can add 15g (½ oz) of butter to the stock at the end for an extra rich stew. Season.

- To serve, spoon the onion stew on to plates and sit the thighs on top.

Steamed Chicken with Really Quick Béarnaise Sauce

Serves 4

Nothing could be simpler than this dish – it's perfect for a quick lunch and a big seller at the hotel. Serve it with noodles, new potatoes, a crisp green salad, or just on its own.

4 large skinless chicken breast fillets, about 150g (5½ oz) each

melted butter, to grease

salt and freshly ground black pepper

1 quantity hollandaise sauce, see page 14

3 tbsp tarragon vinegar

2 tbsp chopped fresh tarragon

- Cut out two pieces of foil, just large enough for two chicken fillets to fit snugly on each one. Butter the foil well, sit two chicken fillets on each piece of foil and season.

- Place a steamer above a pan filled with boiling water – the water should not boil too fiercely, just keep ticking over. Place a piece of foil with its two chicken fillets in each of two steamer baskets and stack one on top of the other on the pan. Cover with the steamer lid. Steam for 20–25 minutes, or until the chicken is cooked through, swapping the baskets around halfway through cooking. The chicken pieces are cooked when they are firm to the touch but with no signs of pinkness; if they still feel soft, steam for a few minutes longer.

- Meanwhile, make the hollandaise sauce as on page 14, substituting the tarragon vinegar for the white wine vinegar. Stir the chopped tarragon into the sauce and season.

- Slice the cooked chicken diagonally into thick slices and spoon over the sauce.

Quick Chicken Stew with Tarragon

Serves 4

4 chicken breast fillets – no skin or bones – about 150g (5½ oz) each

25g (1 oz) butter

1 large leek, trimmed, sliced and washed

1 red onion, finely sliced

125ml (4 fl oz) dry white wine

284ml pot fresh chicken stock

200ml (7 fl oz) double cream

1 tsp wholegrain mustard

1½ tbsp chopped fresh tarragon

salt and freshly ground black pepper

½ lemon

- Cut the chicken into 2½cm (1 in) cubes. Heat the butter in a pan, add the leek and onion and cook gently until softened. Remove the vegetables from the pan using a slotted spoon and keep warm on a plate.

- Add the chicken to the pan and cook quickly to brown all over. Pour the wine and stock into the pan with the chicken and bring to the boil, then reduce the heat and simmer for about 15 minutes, or until the chicken is cooked through.

- When the chicken is cooked, return the leek and onion to the pan, together with the cream, mustard and tarragon, stir and season, then simmer for a further 5 minutes. Add a squeeze of lemon juice to taste, spoon the stew into bowls and serve with boiled new potatoes.

Roast Duck Breast with Green Peppercorns and Apricots

Serves 4

Most people serve duck with thick, heavy, greasy sauces, but here the natural fattiness of the duck is offset by a sweet and sour fruity sauce, sharpened with green peppercorns. If you like, you can also add a touch of sherry or balsamic vinegar to sharpen it even more.

---

4 large duck breasts

2 tsp Chinese five spice powder

385g can apricots in syrup

lemon juice, to taste

salt and freshly ground black pepper

2 tsp green peppercorns in brine

1 tbsp vegetable oil

- Lay the duck breasts flat on a chopping board, skin side up, and use a sharp knife to slash the skin diagonally in both directions. Rub in the Chinese five spice powder and allow to marinate for 1 hour.

- Meanwhile, liquidize the apricots with their syrup and add lemon juice to taste. Season well with salt and pepper. Spoon the mixture into a bowl and add the peppercorns in brine. This takes the sweet edge off the apricots.

- Season the duck. Heat the oil in a large frying pan then add the duck, skin side down, and cook for a few minutes, until the skin is brown and crispy (there will be a fantastic aroma of spices wafting around the kitchen). Turn the duck over, reduce the heat slightly and cook slowly on the other side for about 10 minutes, or until just cooked through. Cover the duck with foil and allow to rest for 2–3 minutes.

- To serve, carve each duck breast diagonally into four to five slices, lay on a plate, overlapping slightly, and spoon a little of the apricot sauce over the top.

Grilled Pork Chops with Blue Cheese Mayo and Shoestring Chips

Serves 4

All pork joints are great value for money. Pork is a very versatile meat and, contrary to popular belief, it's also very low in fat (extra lean pork has even less fat than cottage cheese).

I'm very lucky to have people who supply me with rare old breeds for the hotel: Anne and Kieran from the Bell and Birdtable in Wellington, Somerset produce Oxford Sandy and Black pork, which has the best crackling I've ever tasted, and Simon and Charlotte from Amersham produce Gloucester Old Spot pork, which has great flavour and is very succulent.

800g (1 lb 12 oz) potatoes, peeled
225g (8 oz) mayonnaise
1 small shallot, finely chopped
115g (4 oz) Stilton, crumbled
finely grated zest and juice of $\frac{1}{2}$ lemon
salt and freshly ground black pepper
1 tbsp vegetable oil, plus extra for deep frying
4 pork chops, rind removed

- Preheat the grill to medium high. Cut the potatoes into slices 5mm ($\frac{1}{4}$ in) thick, then cut into long chips 5mm ($\frac{1}{4}$ in) wide and place in a bowl of cold water for about 20–30 minutes.

- Mix together the mayonnaise, shallot, blue stilton and lemon zest, season, add a little lemon juice to taste, then allow to stand at room temperature so that the flavours can mingle.

- Brush a little oil over the chops and season well. Place under the grill and cook slowly for about 5–8 minutes on each side, or until the meat is cooked through and the fat is crispy and golden – remember, if you cook them too quickly they will dry out and become tough. When cooked, allow to rest for 10 minutes so that the meat relaxes and tenderizes.

- Meanwhile, fill a deep pan one-third full with vegetable oil (or use a deep fat fryer) and heat to 150°–170°C (300°–330°F). Drain the soaked chips well, then dry using kitchen paper. Deep-fry the chips for a few minutes, until soft and just pale golden, then remove from the oil. Heat the oil again to bring the temperature to 185°C (355°F), return the chips to the oil and cook until golden brown. Drain on kitchen paper and season well.

- Serve the chops with the chips and the mayonnaise.

Baked Ham with Guinness and Honey

Serves 4

Another one of my favourite dishes, baked ham is very versatile – unglazed it works well when served with noodles and wholegrain mustard cream, and the hocks, cooked in exactly the same way, make a superb salad served with a mustardy dressing. Don't forget to keep the stock to use as a base for classic soups like pea and ham, lentil or butter bean.

750g (1 lb 10 oz) piece gammon collar, salted

1 large onion, sliced

2 carrots, chopped

2 sprigs fresh thyme

2 cloves garlic

12 black peppercorns

2 tsp caster sugar

1 tsp salt

450ml (16 fl oz) Guinness

55g (2 oz) runny honey

115g (4 oz) demerara sugar

- Wash the ham well and place in a large pan. Pour on enough cold water to cover, add the onion, carrots, thyme, garlic, peppercorns, caster sugar and salt and bring to the boil. When the pan is boiling, reduce the heat so that it simmers very gently and cook for exactly 2½ hours. (You may need to top up the liquid with boiling water from a kettle during the cooking time.) At the end of this time, remove from the heat and allow to cool in the liquor for about 45 minutes.

- Preheat the oven to 220°C/425°F/Gas 7. Carefully take the ham out of the liquor and remove any string and the rind. Using a sharp knife, make diagonal slashes in the fat in opposite directions so you get a neat diamond pattern.

- Place on a baking sheet with the fat uppermost (you may need to cut a thin slice from the bottom so that it stands up securely), then pour over the Guinness, drizzle over the honey and sprinkle on the demerara sugar. Cook in the oven for about 20 minutes, basting occasionally with the juices, or until the whole joint has glazed, but do not allow it to burn.

- When nicely glazed, take the ham out of the dish and carve into thick slices. Serve with boiled new potatoes or mash.

Braised Spicy Sausages with Onion Rings and Crushed Potatoes

Serves 4

The cuisine of almost every country in the world includes some variety of sausages. Once seen as a poor man's dish, sausages are now very trendy – they come in exciting flavours and there are more and more companies setting up in the sausage business.

Use spicy sausages for this dish – you can even use the fiery Spanish chorizo variety if you like them, but be careful, as they are very hot and also have quite a lot of fat in them, so they can end up rather greasy. This dish gives a new twist to sausage and mash.

2 tbsp vegetable oil, plus extra for deep frying

8 plump spicy sausages

2 cloves garlic, crushed

200ml (7 fl oz) red wine

2 tsp fresh thyme leaves

large pinch of caster sugar

400ml (14 fl oz) hot beef stock

salt and freshly ground black pepper

4 medium baking potatoes, about 900g (2 lb) total weight

300ml ($\frac{1}{2}$ pint) batter, see page 130

2 tbsp chopped fresh parsley

1 large onion

25g (1 oz) self-raising flour, to dust

1$\frac{1}{2}$ tbsp cornflour

- Preheat the oven to 160°C/325°F/Gas 3. Heat 2 tablespoons of oil in a frying pan. Add the sausages and cook quickly until browned all over, then transfer them to an ovenproof dish, about 1.5 litres (2¾ pints) capacity. Mix the garlic, wine, thyme and sugar into the stock then pour over the sausages. Season, then cover the dish with a tight-fitting lid – if you don't have a lid, you can cover the dish tightly with foil. Cook in the oven for 30–40 minutes, or until the sausages are cooked through.

- Scrub the potatoes well, prick them in several places with a fork or skewer and cook in the microwave on high (650W) for 12–16 minutes, or until tender, then allow to stand for 5 minutes. If you don't have a microwave, you can cook them in the oven for 40 minutes – 1 hour, at 200°C/400°F/Gas 6.

- Add the chopped parsley to the batter. Heat the oil in a deep fat fryer to 180°C (350°F), or fill a deep pan one-third full with oil and use a cooking thermometer to check the temperature. Cut the onion into thick slices and separate into rings a couple of layers thick. Dust the onion rings in a little flour then dip in the batter to coat. Deep-fry the onion rings for about 2 minutes, or until golden brown and crisp. Remove from the oil and drain on kitchen paper, then season with salt.

- When cooked, remove the sausages from the dish and keep warm. Pour the juices into a large pan and boil rapidly for 5 minutes to reduce by about one-third. Stir a little cold water into the cornflour to make a paste, then stir into the reduced stock. Bring back to the boil, stirring continually to thicken.

- Cut each potato into quarters, then cut each piece in half again to make wedges and crush lightly using a potato masher. Place the potatoes in the middle of each plate, top with the sausages and pour over the gravy. Sit the onion rings on top.

Roast Shoulder of Lamb with Pumpkin and Sweet Potatoes

Serves 4–6

I use lamb shoulders a lot, and I sometimes choose hogget, which is a lamb that's over a year old – the meat is darker and more fully flavoured. For this dish, lamb is fine; the main thing is that it has to be very slightly overcooked, so if you're late back from your Sunday lunchtime drink, an extra half an hour will make no difference. Within reason, the meat will stay juicy and moist all the way through, especially if it has a bit of natural fat on it, as this helps to keep it succulent.

3–4 tbsp vegetable oil

2 tbsp redcurrant jelly

2 tsp English mustard powder

1 shoulder of English lamb, about 1.5kg
(3 lb 5 oz)

2 cloves garlic

a few small fresh rosemary sprigs

900g (2 lb) pumpkin, seeds removed

3 sweet potatoes, peeled

salt and freshly ground black pepper

1½ tbsp plain flour

450ml (16 fl oz) beef stock

- Preheat the oven to 160°C/325°F/Gas 3. Pour the oil into a large roasting pan and place in the oven to heat. Mix together the jelly and mustard powder and spread all over the lamb. Cut the garlic into slivers then, using a small sharp knife, make small incisions 2cm (¾ in) deep in the lamb and insert the garlic slivers and rosemary sprigs.

- Cut the pumpkin into three wedges, then cut each wedge into four pieces to make chunks, leaving the skin on. Cut the sweet potatoes in half lengthways then in half again, to make fat wedges. Add the vegetables to the roasting pan and turn to coat in the oil, then place the lamb in the middle. Season the meat and vegetables well.

- Cook in the oven for about 2 hours, turning the pumpkin and sweet potatoes over occasionally – they will soak up and absorb the wonderful lamb juices. If you don't have a roasting tin large enough to hold both the meat and vegetables, you can roast some of the veg in a separate tin – just spoon some of the lamb juices over them during cooking. If the vegetables around the lamb seem a bit too soggy, you can cook them in a separate tin for the last 40 minutes or so to crisp them up a bit.

- To serve, lift the lamb out of the tin, place on a large warm plate and surround with the pumpkin and sweet potatoes. Cover with foil and allow to rest for about 15 minutes.

- To make the gravy, tip any excess fat out of the roasting tin, leaving about 3 tablespoons of the tasty lamb juices and those lovely crispy bits of lamb and vegetables in the tin. Add the flour and stir in, then add the beef stock and bring to the boil, stirring. Simmer for 2–3 minutes, then check the seasoning and add a little mint jelly to taste, if you like. Serve the gravy with the lamb.

Lamb Shank Stew with Chick Peas and Rosemary

Serves 4

My best mate Paul Vidic first cooked a navarin of lamb for me. It was delicious and so I've recreated his recipe here, using shanks.

I love stews that have lots of vegetables and very little stock – the flavour is so intense and powerful. This stew is a complete meal on its own.

2 large lamb shanks

3 large sprigs fresh rosemary

2 cloves garlic, crushed

4 tbsp olive oil

1 onion, peeled and cut into wedges

1 parsnip, peeled and cut into chunks

4 carrots, peeled and cut into chunks

salt and freshly ground black pepper

1 chicken stock cube

4 tsp plain flour

1 tbsp tomato purée

4 tsp mint jelly

5 tsp Worcestershire sauce

2 tsp white wine vinegar

410g can chick peas, drained

- Place the lamb, rosemary, garlic and 2 tablespoons of the oil in a large bowl and turn to coat in the oil. Add the onion, parsnip, carrots and seasoning and allow to stand for at least 2 hours to marinate.

- Preheat the oven to 160°C/325°F/Gas 3. Dissolve the stock cube in 600ml (1 pint) of boiling water. Heat the remaining oil in a large frying pan. Add the lamb and cook quickly on both sides to brown, then add the rosemary and allow to wilt – the kitchen will be filled with the wonderful aroma of the rosemary. Remove the shanks and the rosemary from the pan and place in a large casserole dish with the vegetables and seasoning.

- Add the flour and the tomato purée to the frying pan and stir well to soak up the oil, then pour in the stock and bring to the boil, stirring. Add the mint jelly, Worcestershire sauce and vinegar to the stock, pour into the casserole dish, cover with a tight-fitting lid and cook in the oven for 1½ hours. After this time, remove the lid and stir in the chick peas, then continue to cook in the oven, uncovered, for a further 30 minutes, or until the lamb is tender, soft and succulent.

Mustard Roast Beef with Yorkshire Pudding and Onion Gravy

Serves 4

All through the BSE beef crisis, the Castle continued to use British beef and was proud to do so. We only use 18-month-old steer meat, and our sales of roast beef on Sundays never dwindled.

I know everyone has their own recipe for roast beef, but here's my version, with Yorkshire pud and gravy. The secret of Yorkshire puddings is to start them in hot oil in a hot tray in a hot oven – then they will rise and set perfectly. Like croissants and some yeast-based food, Yorkshire puds are best cooked, left to cool then heated again just before serving.

---

vegetable oil, for greasing

900g (2 lb) piece well-hung sirloin British beef

salt and freshly ground black pepper

2 tbsp English mustard powder

For the Yorkshire pudding:

4 eggs

600ml (1 pint) milk

225g (8 oz) plain flour

salt and freshly ground black pepper

For the gravy:

3 large onions, sliced

2 cloves garlic, crushed

250ml (9 fl oz) red wine

2 beef stock cubes

dash of Worcestershire sauce

- Preheat the oven to 200°C/400°F/Gas 6. Grease each compartment of a twelve-hole Yorkshire pudding tray with a little oil. Rub the beef all over with plenty of salt and pepper and the mustard powder. Scrunch up a large piece of foil and place in a roasting pan, flattening out slightly, then sit the beef on top (the foil helps to keep the beef off the bottom of the baking tray). Place the beef in the oven with the Yorkshire pudding tin and cook for 10 minutes.

- To make the Yorkshire pudding, crack the eggs into a bowl, add 150ml (¼ pint) of the milk and whisk together, then add the flour and mix to a smooth batter with the rest of the milk – do not season until the last minute.

- Remove the Yorkshire pudding tin from the oven and reduce the heat to 160°C/325°F/Gas 3. Set a timer for the beef – cook for a further 30–35 minutes for a rare result, but if you prefer your beef well done, add an additional 25–35 minutes.

- Meanwhile, pour the Yorkshire pudding batter into the preheated tin and immediately return to the oven to cook alongside the beef. Cook the Yorkshire pudding until well risen and golden brown, approximately 20–25 minutes. Take out of the oven and leave to cool. When cooked to taste, remove the meat from the oven, cover with foil and allow to rest for 15–20 minutes.

- To make the onion gravy, place all the ingredients in a pan with 425ml (15 fl oz) of water. Bring to the boil, stirring, then simmer rapidly until well reduced to a thick sauce.

- Before you are ready to serve, pop the Yorkshire pudding back into the oven for a few minutes to warm through.

- Carve the beef into slices and serve with the Yorkshire pudding and your choice of roast vegetables, then pour over the onion gravy.

Greens, Salads and Vegetables

Smoked Chicken Salad with Lentils and Walnut Oil

The only major thing to do here is to make the lentil dressing – it is a bit time-consuming, but worth it.

Now, a word about salad leaves. We chefs are notorious for saying 'In my restaurant we use . . .' We are fortunate in having access to growers but, assuming you don't, try and balance your leaves – red radicchio is very bitter so look for something different like lamb's lettuce and pak choi which are great in salads, or even baby spinach. If you can, steer clear of lollo rosso and iceberg – they are good in certain things, but be adventurous and experiment.

300ml (½ pint) hot chicken stock
2 small shallots, finely chopped
55g (2 oz) dried red lentils
2 tsp Dijon mustard
2 tsp sherry or white wine vinegar
salt and freshly ground black pepper
pinch of caster sugar
100–125ml (3½–4 fl oz) vegetable oil
dash of walnut oil
200g (7 oz) mixed salad leaves
4 boneless smoked chicken breasts

- Place the chicken stock in a pan, add the shallots and bring to the boil, then reduce the heat so that the liquid simmers slowly. Meanwhile, rinse the lentils under cold running water and give them a good wash, then add to the simmering stock and cook for about 10–15 minutes, or until the lentils are soft and cooked.

- Once cooked, tip the lentils and stock into a blender and blitz until smooth and velvety. Strain through a fine sieve into a bowl, add the mustard and vinegar and mix together thoroughly. Season and add a pinch of sugar to taste. Allow to cool.

- Gradually whisk the vegetable oil into the cooled mixture (lentils can vary, so the exact amount of oil you need will depend on the type of lentils used – some will make a thicker mixture than others). Add a dash of walnut oil to taste (be careful though, it's powerful stuff!). Adjust the seasoning again if necessary.

- Place the salad leaves in a large bowl. Cut the chicken into slices on a slight angle and arrange on a large plate. Spoon a little dressing over the chicken then spoon a little more of the dressing over the salad leaves and season. Pile the leaves next to the chicken and serve. This salad works well with boiled new potatoes and crusty bread.

Sweet Potato and Corn Chowder

Serves 4

I rather like the way the Americans go about their cooking. In some ways, good food is still new to them and they are therefore very enthusiastic about it. If only they could overcome their insatiable appetite for junk, their cuisine would have a wonderful reputation.

The chowder you get in the States is fantastic when cooked well. Here is my version, which is a cross between a soup and a casserole.

3 tbsp vegetable oil

2 small onions, finely chopped

1 clove garlic, crushed

55g (2 oz) plain flour

600ml (1 pint) hot chicken or vegetable stock

340g can sweetcorn niblets, drained

pinch of sugar

salt and freshly ground black pepper

3 medium sweet potatoes, peeled

2 tbsp roughly chopped fresh parsley

150ml (¼ pint) double cream

- Heat the vegetable oil in a large pan, add the onions and garlic and cook gently for about 5 minutes, or until softened. Remove the pan from the heat and stir in the flour, then add the stock, little by little, stirring continuously. Return the pan to the heat and bring to a simmer, still stirring so that the sauce does not catch on the bottom. Add the sweetcorn and sugar and season.

- Meanwhile, cut the sweet potatoes into 2cm (¾ in) cubes then add to the hot soup. Bring back to a simmer and cover the pan with a tight-fitting lid, or use a piece of foil and cover tightly. Simmer for about 20–25 minutes, or until the sweet potatoes are tender. Stir occasionally.

- When cooked, stir in the parsley and cream and season again. Ladle the soup into deep bowls and serve with crusty brown bread.

Roast Pumpkin with Garlic Butter and Sage

The first time I had roast pumpkin was in New Zealand and it was delicious. Until then I had never really cared much for pumpkin – it had always tasted pretty bland. But I now know that when it's roasted with garlic and sage, two big flavours that really enhance it, pumpkin makes a perfect accompaniment for any roast meat. You can also cook it around a roast joint so that it absorbs the roasting juices (see *Roast lamb and sweet potatoes*, page 92).

4 cloves garlic, crushed

1 tsp crushed black peppercorns

about 10 fresh sage leaves, finely chopped

sea salt

175g (6 oz) butter, softened

about 1.25kg (2 lb 12 oz) pumpkin – the most common varieties are Crown Prince or New Zealand

⬭ Preheat the oven to 190°C/375°F/Gas 5.

⬭ Add the garlic, peppercorns and sage to the softened butter with a few pinches of sea salt and mix really well.

⬭ Scoop the seeds out of the pumpkin and remove any pith and rough stringy flesh (in the same way that you would prepare a melon). Cut into about sixteen evenly sized chunks, leaving the skin on. Place the pumpkin in a roasting tin and spread a little of the garlic butter on to each piece. Cook in the oven for about 50 minutes to 1 hour, or until tender and browned – keep spooning over the buttery juices and turn the pumpkin over occasionally. Serve straightaway.

Twenty-minute Braised Cabbage with Bacon and Onions

Serves 4

Cabbage is one of my favourite vegetables – it is so versatile and tasty, and with a little care and attention you can make some top dishes. Baby spring greens also work well in this recipe.

175g (6 oz) unsalted butter
2 small red onions, sliced
6 rashers smoked back bacon, thinly sliced
1 small savoy cabbage
salt and freshly ground black pepper

- Heat the butter in a large pan until it starts to bubble (but do not brown), then add the onion and bacon and cook, stirring, for about 5 minutes.

- While the onions and bacon are cooking, remove all the outside leaves from the cabbage and discard. Cut the remaining cabbage into quarters and shred very thinly. Wash well and drain thoroughly.

- Add the cabbage to the bacon and onions and stir, then cover with a tight-fitting lid and cook for a further 15 minutes, stirring occasionally. The cabbage will stew in the butter and the retained moisture.

- At the end of cooking, season, then tip into a large bowl and serve. The buttery juices are delicious; all you need with it is crusty bread and a chunk of cheese.

Hot Wild Mushrooms with Pine Nuts and Parmesan

Serves 4

The term 'wild' mushroom does not strictly apply here, as most of the wild mushrooms you can buy are now cultivated. Of course, if you have the inclination you can get up and go looking for them in the woods, but you need to know exactly what you are doing. I would stick to the local deli or supermarket – it's much easier. Steer clear of dried varieties, unless you're putting them in stews or braises, as they will be too limp and rubbery for this salad.

1 medium cos lettuce
225g (8 oz) grey oyster mushrooms
225g (8 oz) shiitake or blewit mushrooms
115g (4 oz) block Parmesan
1 clove garlic, crushed
½ tsp caster sugar
2 tsp chopped fresh coriander
4 tsp sherry vinegar
3 tbsp olive oil
salt and freshly ground black pepper
2 shallots, finely sliced
3 tbsp vegetable oil
55g (2 oz) pine nuts

- Cut the stalk off the lettuce and wash the leaves. Drain well or use a salad spinner, then cut the leaves into 1cm (½ in) strips across the leaf.

- Pick over the mushrooms and remove any stray bits and pieces of straw, compost etc.

- Cut the Parmesan into thin slices using a vegetable peeler (when you get to the small end, use a coarse grater).

- Place the garlic in a bowl with the sugar, coriander, vinegar and olive oil and mix well. Season, then add the shallots and allow to stand for 1 hour.

- In a large frying pan or wok, heat the vegetable oil for a couple of minutes, then add the mushrooms and season well. Stir around so that they cook very quickly – it's important you don't overcook them – then add the pine nuts and stir in.

- Place the lettuce in a large bowl, season, pour over some of the shallot dressing and toss. Tip the entire contents of the frying pan or wok over the lettuce and stir well. Serve immediately, before it goes too limp, scattering over the Parmesan shavings.

Nettle Soup with Onions and Chick Peas

Serves 4–6

Nettles are an unusual ingredient but they make a good soup. The Italians combine them with ricotta cheese to stuff pancakes, and the French love them in soups and tarts. The Victorians used nettles in tea for the invigorating feeling they were believed to give. Apart from making a great soup, this recipe also solves the problem of the early spring growth of nettle shoots in the garden.

You should use nettles that are no more than 15–18cm (6–7 in) high and have branched three times. Throw the stalks away and only use the leaves – don't forget to use rubber gloves when you're handling or picking them.

350g (12 oz) nettles (about half a supermarket bag full)

2 tbsp vegetable oil

2 large onions, chopped

1 small leek, chopped

2 sticks celery, chopped

1 large baking potato, peeled

1.2 litres (2 pints) hot fresh chicken or vegetable stock

2 × 400g can chick peas, drained

salt and freshly ground black pepper

- Pull the leaves off the nettles and discard the stalks. Wash the leaves well.

- Heat the oil in a large pan then add the onions, leek and celery and cook gently until they have softened. Do not allow to colour.

- Cut the potato into 6–8 chunks and add to the pan, together with the stock and a quarter of the chick peas. Bring to the boil and simmer for 15 minutes, or until the potatoes are tender.

- Add the nettles to the soup. Stir and simmer for a further 5 minutes, or until they break down. Pour the soup into a blender (you may need to do this in batches) and blitz until smooth; then, if you want to, pass the soup through a sieve and return to the pan. Add the remaining chick peas, season well and heat through. Serve piping hot in bowls.

Stuffed Peppers with Basil Breadcrumbs and Saffron Mayo

Serves 4

You must make sure that the peppers you use for this dish have flat bottoms. This will ensure that they will stand up when they are cooked. I love peppers – they are delicious in salads and stir-fries and also make cracking good soups and sauces. Their natural shape means they are ideal for stuffing and then baking or roasting. This dish is always popular in the Brasserie, especially at lunchtime.

40g (1½ oz) long grain rice

3 large red peppers

2 large yellow peppers

1 onion

1 courgette

3 tbsp olive oil

2 cloves garlic, crushed

2 tbsp chopped fresh basil

zest of ½ lemon, finely grated

salt and freshly ground black pepper

25g (1 oz) butter

25g (1 oz) white bread

25g (1 oz) Parmesan, freshly grated

saffron mayo, to serve, see page 107

- Preheat the oven to 220°C/425°F/Gas 7. Cook the rice in a pan of boiling salted water until tender, then drain.

- Cut one of the red peppers in half, remove the seeds and cut the flesh into 1cm (½ in) cubes. Cut the tops off the remaining peppers, about 1cm (½ in) from the top, and chop the tops into cubes. Scoop the seeds out of the peppers using a spoon, and discard.

- Cut the onion and courgette into 1cm (½ in) cubes. Heat the oil in a pan until just smoking, then add the onion, courgette, chopped pepper, garlic and half the basil. Turn down the heat and cook gently for a few minutes, until softened. Add the lemon zest and season well.

- Remove the pan from the heat and stir in the cooked rice, then use this mixture to fill the remaining peppers.

- Sit the peppers in a deep ovenproof dish, placing a knob of butter on top of each one, and pour in enough cold water to come about 2cm (¾ in) up the sides of the dish. Cover the dish with a lid or a piece of foil and cook in the oven for about 35–40 minutes, or until the peppers are tender – you should be able to push a skewer or small sharp knife easily through the pepper flesh.

- Meanwhile, place the bread in a mini food processor and blitz, to make rough breadcrumbs. Add the remaining basil and season, then blitz again briefly. Add the Parmesan to the breadcrumbs and mix together.

- Take the foil off the cooked peppers and top each with equal amounts of the breadcrumbs. Place the dish back in the oven, uncovered, for a few minutes, until the breadcrumbs are golden brown (be careful, as they can burn quickly). Serve with saffron mayonnaise.

103

Grilled Goat's Cheese with Apples and Chive Oil

Serves 4

Here in the West Country, we are blessed with some of the best cheeses in the whole of the United Kingdom and I try to make full use of them in the restaurant. Even the cheeseboard includes only good old British cheeses.

A few years ago I discovered Capricorn Goat's Cheese, produced in Crewkerne in Somerset. It's perfect for cooking, as it melts quickly while holding together well. However, any goat's cheese would be fine in this recipe.

If you prefer, the apples can be replaced with ripe, juicy pears, but remember to remove their cores (good varieties include William, Bartlett or Bon Cretion).

This recipe can be served as a starter or as a main course.

16 small potatoes, scrubbed clean
3 tbsp olive oil, plus a little extra for drizzling
1 tsp wholegrain mustard
2 tbsp roughly chopped fresh chives
pinch of caster sugar
2 tbsp finely chopped fresh chives
salt and freshly ground black pepper
$\frac{1}{2}$ lemon
4 small, soft goat's cheeses
selection of salad leaves, about 300g (10$\frac{1}{2}$ oz)
3 Granny Smith apples

- Preheat the grill to high.

- Cook the potatoes in a pan of boiling water until tender. Drain, then cut in half lengthways.

- Place the oil, mustard, roughly chopped chives and sugar in a mini food processor, season, then blitz until smooth. Pass the mixture through a sieve into a bowl and stir in the finely chopped chives. Check the seasoning and keep at room temperature. If you want to, you can add a squeeze of lemon juice at the last minute, but it may spoil the brilliant green colour of the dressing. Alternatively, you can drizzle a little lemon juice over the salad leaves.

- Cut the goat's cheeses in half horizontally and place on a baking sheet. Season well and drizzle over a little olive oil. Place under the grill and just warm through – don't overcook or you will melt them and not be able to lift them up.

- Arrange the potatoes around the edge of a large serving plate. Place the salad leaves in a bowl, season and add a little of the chive dressing, then toss to coat lightly. Pile the salad into the middle of the plate. Cut each apple into 6–8 thin wedges, remove the cores and arrange around the salad, then sit the cheese on top of the leaves. Serve straightaway with the rest of the dressing.

Flat Mushroom and Beetroot Salad with Creamy Garlic Dressing

Serves 4–6 as an accompaniment

This beetroot salad is delicious with deep-fried fish or even rare roast lamb. A lot of people don't like beetroot, most probably because they have only eaten the pickled variety, but increasingly supermarkets are stocking fresh beetroot. My local doctor grows five or six varieties for me, from yellow to red and white ringed, and they are fabulous.

4 medium raw, fresh beetroot

salt and freshly ground black pepper

2 tsp chopped fresh basil

olive oil, to drizzle

8 large flat mushrooms

85g (3 oz) lamb's lettuce

2 tsp Dijon mustard

2 tbsp white wine vinegar

2 cloves garlic, crushed

300ml (½ pint) vegetable oil

150ml (¼ pint) whipping cream

- Preheat the grill to high.

- Give the beetroot a really good wash and scrub off any excess mud and grit. Place in a pan, stalk end down and with the long root intact (otherwise the beetroot will 'bleed' and leave all their colour in the cooking water). Pour on enough cold water to cover and add a little salt. Bring to the boil then reduce the heat and simmer until tender – this will take about 50 minutes to 1 hour. Drain and allow the beetroot to cool.

- Once cooled, peel the beetroot carefully and cut into any shape you want – I like wedges. Place in a large bowl, season, add the basil and a dash of olive oil, stir well and allow to stand for 2–3 hours if possible.

- Lay the flat mushrooms on a baking sheet – if they are very large you may need to use two baking sheets. Season well and drizzle over a generous amount of olive oil, then cook under the grill until lightly browned and slightly shrunk – grilling seems to make them very firm and 'meaty'. Turn and grill the other side. Drizzle over a little more olive oil and leave to stand and marinate.

- Check over the lamb's lettuce to make sure there is no 'wildlife' or dirt, then make the dressing: place the mustard, vinegar and garlic in a bowl, season and, with a balloon whisk, whisk together. Gradually add in the vegetable oil in a thin stream, whisking all the time so the dressing thickens and comes together. Whisk in the cream then check the seasoning.

- To serve, cut the mushrooms into segments and arrange on a plate with the beetroot. Pile the lamb's lettuce in the middle and spoon over the garlic dressing.

Warm Potato Salad with Rocket, Watercress and Saffron Mayonnaise

Serves 4

This salad is very good to eat on its own but I sometimes serve it as a side salad with roast cod or shark. It is impressive to look at and tastes delicious.

4 large baking potatoes
2 pinches saffron strands
200g (7 oz) ready-made mayonnaise
pinch of ground saffron powder
4 tsp chopped chives
3 shallots, finely chopped
salt and freshly ground black pepper
2 bunches watercress
100g (3½ oz) rocket leaves

Wash the potatoes well to remove any grit and mud, then place in a large pan of boiling water and cook until they are tender. Place the pan under a cold running tap to cool the potatoes slightly, then peel using a small sharp knife. (You can peel them while they're hot if you want, but you'll have to wear your Marigolds!) Cut the potatoes into 1½cm (⅝ in) cubes, place in a bowl and cover with clingfilm to keep warm.

Place the saffron strands in a small bowl, add 2 teaspoons of boiling water and allow to stand for 5 minutes. Mix the soaked saffron strands into the mayonnaise, together with the saffron powder, chives and shallots, then season. If you like, you can add a little mustard or vinegar.

Discard any brown leaves or stalks from the watercress and rocket and wash the leaves well. Drain the leaves and pat dry in a clean tea-towel. (If you want to be flash, invest in a salad spinner, they're great for drying leaves.)

To finish, mix the watercress and rocket together and season. Fold the potatoes into the saffron mayonnaise, check the seasoning and adjust if necessary. Spoon the potato salad into the middle of the plates and pile the leaves on top. Serve with crusty bread.

Oven-dried Tomatoes

Serves 4 as an accompaniment

I wish I didn't have to use tomatoes in the winter when they are more often than not tasteless. Thankfully, in recent years supermarkets seem to be cottoning on to the fact that taste is more important than looks.

If you do use tomatoes in winter, or even summer for that matter, the way to cook them is to 'dry bake' them, so the natural sugar intensifies and they are still juicy. Serve as a summer starter or with any type of mash (see the potato chapter).

8 ripe plum tomatoes, or vine tomatoes

3 tbsp balsamic vinegar

2 tbsp good olive oil

15g (½ oz) caster sugar

salt and freshly ground black pepper

- Preheat the oven to 140°C/275°F/Gas 1.

- Cut the tomatoes in half lengthways. Place a wire cooling rack securely on top of a shallow baking tin and arrange the tomatoes closely together on top, cut side up. In a bowl, stir together the vinegar, olive oil and caster sugar until the sugar has dissolved, then spoon the mixture over the tomatoes. Bake in the oven for about 4–5 hours, or until the tomatoes have shrunk in size by about half.

Roast Red Onions with Crunchy Cheddar Topping

Serves 4

Over the past few years red onions have become fashionable and most supermarkets now sell them. Plain roasted around the Sunday joint, they make a super accompaniment to roast duck and lamb. They also make great marmalade, a base for good chutneys and are also delicious used raw, sliced into salads.

8 medium red onions, with skins

1 egg

4 slices brown bread

2 cloves garlic, crushed

salt and freshly ground black pepper

175g (6 oz) mature Cheddar, cut into 5mm (¼ in) cubes

25g (1 oz) unsalted butter

2 tsp wholegrain mustard

pinch of caster sugar

- Preheat the oven to 200°C/400°F/Gas 6. Scrunch up a piece of foil and place in a baking tin then sit the onions on top, to prevent them from burning on the bottom. Cook in the oven for about 2 hours, or until the onions are very tender – you should be able to push a skewer through them without any resistance. Remove from the oven and allow to cool.

- Cook the egg in a pan of boiling water for 8–10 minutes to hard boil, then place the pan under cold running water for 5 minutes to cool the egg. Peel the egg, then use a wooden spoon to press it through a sieve and into a large bowl.

- Place the bread in a food processor and blitz to make rough breadcrumbs, then add the garlic, season and blitz for another minute. Add the breadcrumbs and the cheese to the egg and mix well.

- Carefully peel the outer two or three layers off the onions, so you are left with the soft flesh. Cut the onions in half lengthways through the root and place on kitchen paper, cut side down, to drain.

- Heat the butter in a large frying pan until it begins to foam. Meanwhile, spread a little mustard over the cut edge of each onion half and season with salt, pepper and a pinch of sugar. Add the onions to the butter, cut side down, and cook gently until the onions are caramelized and browned.

- Increase the oven temperature to 220°C/425°F/Gas 7. Carefully transfer the onions to a baking tin, sprinkle some of the breadcrumbs over each one and bake for about 15 minutes, or until the topping is nicely glazed and melted.

Spinach and Wild Rice Cakes with Cherry Tomato Dressing

Serves 4

100g (3½ oz) wild rice

500g (1 lb 2 oz) spinach, cooked

675g (1½ lb) potatoes, peeled (use Maris Piper or any good mashing potatoes)

3 tbsp olive oil

2 medium onions, chopped

3 cloves garlic, crushed

1 tbsp chopped fresh dill

2 eggs, beaten

salt and freshly ground black pepper

200g (7 oz) dry breadcrumbs

vegetable oil, for frying

For the cherry tomato dressing:

1 plum tomato

250g (9 oz) cherry tomatoes, cut in half

2 tsp balsamic vinegar

150ml (¼ pint) vegetable oil

3 tbsp extra virgin olive oil

½ lemon

salt and freshly ground black pepper

- Cook the wild rice in a pan of boiling water until tender. Drain and allow to cool.

- Heat a large pan, add the spinach and 3 tablespoons of water and stir over a fairly high heat until the spinach has wilted. Drain the spinach and squeeze out any excess moisture, then roughly chop.

- Cut the potatoes into evenly sized pieces, then cook in a pan of boiling salted water until tender. Drain, then return to the pan and place over a low heat to drive off any excess moisture. (Be careful not to stir the potatoes too much or they may become gluey.) Break up with a potato masher and keep warm.

- Meanwhile, heat the olive oil in a frying pan, add the onions and garlic and cook gently until softened, but do not allow to brown.

- Place the onions in a large bowl, add the dill, rice and spinach and mix together carefully. Add the mash and 2 tablespoons of beaten egg, season well and mix again, adding just enough of the breadcrumbs to make a stiff dough. Shape the mixture into eight balls then slightly flatten out into cakes. Chill for about 1 hour.

- Season the remaining beaten eggs and pour into a shallow dish. Place the remaining breadcrumbs in another shallow dish.

- Dip the cakes in the egg, shake off any excess, then roll them in the breadcrumbs to coat. The cakes will keep in the fridge for 3–4 days, but you may need to re-coat them in breadcrumbs if they have absorbed moisture while in the fridge.

- To cook the cakes, heat a little vegetable oil in a large frying pan, pop in the cakes and cook over a medium heat for about 3–5 minutes on each side, or until they become crunchy and nicely browned. Drain on kitchen paper.

- To make the dressing, cut the plum tomato into quarters and remove the seeds, then place in a food processor with 150g (5½ oz) of the cherry tomatoes, the balsamic vinegar and 50ml (2 fl oz) of water and blitz (don't process for too long or the seeds will break up and make the dressing bitter). With the motor still running, add the oils very slowly through the lid to make a thick dressing. Press the dressing through a sieve into a bowl, add the remaining cherry tomatoes and a squeeze of lemon juice and season.

- Serve the cakes with a green salad and the cherry tomato dressing.

Quick Butter Bean Soup with Thyme and Olive Oil

Serves 4

Certain tinned pulses, for example split peas, haricot and borlotti beans, are extremely good in soups, braises and stews. Dried beans are fine, but you have to soak them overnight and cook them properly, which can be a chore.

I once cooked this soup for a very well-known chef/ writer. He liked it so much he had two bowls, so it must be good!

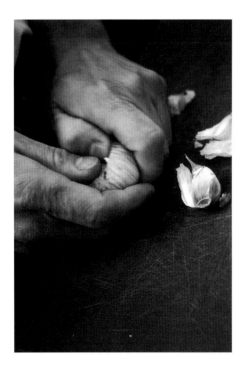

4 tsp vegetable oil

2 small onions, chopped

1 small leek, chopped, well washed and drained

2 cloves garlic, crushed

about 1.2 litres (2 pints) hot chicken or vegetable stock

2 × 420g cans butter beans, drained

pinch of medium curry powder

2 tsp fresh thyme leaves

salt and freshly ground black pepper

dash of milk, optional

olive oil, to drizzle

- Heat the vegetable oil in a large pan, then add the onion, leek and garlic and cook gently until they are tender and golden brown. Do not allow to burn. Add the stock, beans, curry powder and thyme and simmer for about 15–20 minutes, or until all the vegetables are soft and tender.

- Once cooked, pour the soup into a blender and blitz until smooth – you may need to do this in batches – then pour back into the pan, check the seasoning and add a little milk if the soup is too thick.

- Serve the soup in bowls, piping hot. Drizzle a little olive oil over the top and stir in.

Potatoes

Cheesy Chips

I like two types of chips: the fat, semi-soggy ones that come with your fish or a steamed steak pudding and gravy, and the crisp, lovely shoestring ones served in most burger joints these days. They only match certain dishes – crispy chips, for example, work well with burgers, fried fish and peas, grilled pork and lamb chops and with melted cheese and Worcestershire sauce (see recipe below), whereas the fat ones go with meat puddings, gravy, curry sauce and baked beans. For my method of cooking chips, see page 69.

I got the idea for this recipe when I spent a day with the Channel fish boys, Nigel and Martyn (the Castle's suppliers and good friends), for a pool competition and a few large gin and tonics. Halfway through the competition large bowls of fat chips, melted cheese and Worcestershire sauce appeared. With that memory in mind, I started to play around at home and came up with this recipe – perfect for a night in watching the footie!

crispy thin chips

Worcestershire sauce

salt and freshly ground black pepper

tallegio or Cambazola cheese,
cut into thin slices

There's no method here – just crisp-fry the chips, season well with salt, pepper and Worcestershire sauce, then sprinkle over the cheese and melt under a grill.

Sautéed New Potatoes with Broad Beans and Soft Onions

Serves 4 as an accompaniment

A lot of people hate broad beans, although I suspect it's the skins they dislike as they can taste bitter. Here, cooked with soft onions and potatoes, they are delicious.

500g (1 lb 2 oz) baby new potatoes

1 tsp salt

3 medium onions

salt and freshly ground black pepper

125–150ml (4–5 fl oz) olive oil

2.25kg (5 lb) fresh broad beans

55g (2 oz) unsalted butter

- Preheat the oven to 160°C/325°F/Gas 3. Place the potatoes in a large pan, cover with cold water, add 1 teaspoon of salt, then bring to the boil and cook until the potatoes are tender and a knife can be pushed through them with no resistance. Drain the potatoes through a colander and allow to cool.

- Cut the onions into slices 1cm (½ in) thick and lay on a baking sheet. Season well and pour over the olive oil. Place in the preheated oven and cook for about 30 minutes, or until the onions are really soft. Remove from the oven and keep warm.

- Meanwhile, pop open the pods and place the beans in a bowl.

- Bring a large pan of water to the boil and add some salt. Add the beans and bring back to the boil, then immediately strain through a colander. Place under a cold running tap and cool the beans. Once cool, pinch one end of the beans to squeeze out the lovely green insides. Keep them in a bowl. Discard the bitter skins.

- Cut the cooked potatoes in half lengthways. Heat the butter in a wok or large pan. When it is just starting to change colour add the potatoes, season well and cook until they start to brown, stirring occasionally. Toss in the beans and warm through, then spoon on to plates or bowls and top with the onions. This makes an excellent accompaniment for roast chicken or early summer mackerel.

Mash

Mash is, to me, the best thing you can do with a potato. It's such a wonderful creation – soft, silky, smooth and absolutely perfect with most dishes. There's been a lot of press in recent years about mash and it has become very fashionable, but I've been a fan of good mash for ages.

Potatoes are notoriously fickle things to cook. You can make mash with the same variety of potatoes, out of the same bag, using exactly the same method and it can still turn out slightly different every time. I've tried to fathom this out, to no avail, so I now put it down to the fact that potatoes are just contrary.

This is my method for cooking mash, which will hopefully work for you too. The quantities cannot be too accurate as every potato is different, so these are rough guidelines only.

You can then add flavourings as you wish. A few suggestions are:

- finely chopped spring onions for fish, lamb and chicken dishes
- wholegrain mustard for grilled liver and bacon
- chopped parsley for a fish pie topping
- chopped black olives for roast cod
- roasted garlic (cooked in a moderate oven for about 45 minutes, then peeled and chopped)

- Use Maris Piper, Cara, Marfona or even the large waxy baking potatoes. Wash them well, peel, then wash again. You can stop peeled potatoes discolouring by keeping them in a bowl of cold water, but they should only be kept in this way for a maximum of 24 hours.

- Do not cut the potatoes too small; most potatoes I just cut in half. Place in a pan and cover with plenty of water then bring to the boil. Don't add any salt. Once the pan is boiling, reduce the heat to a gentle simmer and leave them just ticking over until you can push a sharp knife right through the potatoes with no resistance. Tip the potatoes into a colander, then return to the pan, reduce the heat to its lowest possible setting and shake the pan over the heat to drive off any excess moisture from the potatoes. Do not stir the potatoes at this point as they can go 'gluey'.

- Push the potatoes through a mouli or potato ricer in small amounts but do not overwork them as this can also make them gluey. If you're using the mash in another recipe, such as potato cakes, don't add any milk or butter.

- If the mash is to be served as an accompaniment, transfer it to a bowl, add a generous amount of salt and pepper and enough milk and butter to make a soft smooth mash, then beat well – I sometimes use a small electric whisk.

Sweetcorn Potato Cakes with Tarragon and Spring Onions

Serves 4 as an accompaniment

I serve potato cakes a lot in the hotel. They go well with anything from duck to chicken and even fish. These potato cakes are simple to make and a good way of using up leftover mash. You can add all sorts of different ingredients and flavourings to them – just let your imagination run riot.

450g (1 lb) plain mashed potato
4 spring onions, chopped
340g can sweetcorn niblets, drained
1 tbsp chopped fresh tarragon
salt and freshly ground black pepper
1 egg yolk
about 6–8 tbsp dry breadcrumbs
3 tbsp vegetable oil

- Place the potato, spring onions, sweetcorn and tarragon in a bowl, season well and mix together. Add the egg yolk and enough breadcrumbs to make a fairly firm mixture. Shape the mixture into eight small balls then flatten to make patties about 1½cm (⅝ in) thick.

- Heat the oil in a non-stick frying pan. Add the potato cakes and cook for a few minutes on each side until golden brown and warmed through.

- These make an excellent accompaniment for scrambled, poached or fried eggs and even fried chicken, see page 26.

Stuffed Potatoes with Gruyère Cheese and Parsnip & Carrot Crisps

Serves 4

This is a perfect light lunch dish, which is quick and easy to make. You can cook the potatoes in the microwave if you like, but then you'll miss out on the crispy skins which are the best bit.

2 large baking potatoes

1 parsnip, peeled

1 large carrot, peeled

vegetable oil, for deep-frying

salt and freshly ground pepper

25g (1 oz) unsalted butter

1 tbsp milk

4 spring onions

115g (4 oz) Gruyère or Emmenthal cheese, cut into 1cm ($\frac{1}{2}$ in) cubes

- Preheat the oven to 200°C/400°F/Gas 6. Prick the potatoes using a fork or skewer and bake in the oven for 1–1$\frac{1}{2}$ hours, or until the potatoes are tender and the skins are dry and crispy.

- Meanwhile, use a potato peeler to cut very thin, long strips off the parsnip and carrot. Heat the oil in a deep fat fryer to 170°C (335°F), or fill a deep saucepan one-third full with oil and use a cooking thermometer to check the temperature as the oil heats up. Fry the parsnip strips for 1–2 minutes, or until light golden brown – the oil will stop bubbling when the parsnips are ready. Lift out the parsnip slices and drain on kitchen paper. Repeat using the carrot strips then allow to cool so that they crisp up nicely. Season.

- Cut the baked potatoes in half and scoop out the centres into a bowl. Add the butter, milk and season. Use a fork to combine and just break up the potato, but don't overmix.

- Chop the spring onions and add to the potato mixture with the cheese, stir together and spoon back into the potato skins. Place the potatoes on a baking sheet and return to the oven for about 5 minutes, or until the cheese is just beginning to melt.

- To serve, place the potatoes on a plate and top with the parsnip and carrot crisps. Branston pickle makes a tasty accompaniment.

My Mum's Half and Half-ers

Serves 4 as an accompaniment

My mum always called these half and half-ers! They make a delicious accompaniment to cold meats and even grilled fish.

> 4 potatoes – Maris Piper or other baking
> potatoes, about 200g (7 oz) each
> vegetable oil, for deep-frying
> salt and freshly ground black pepper

- Peel, then wash the potatoes. Cut them in half lengthways, then cut each piece in half lengthways again to make thin wedges. Cook the potatoes in a pan of boiling water for about 15 minutes, or until just tender. Drain well and allow to cool for 5 minutes.

- Heat the oil in a deep fat fryer to 190°C (375°F), or use a deep saucepan filled one-third full with oil. Add the potatoes and cook for 5–6 minutes until they are nicely browned and the edges are crispy. Remove the potatoes from the oil and drain on kitchen paper, then sprinkle with salt and pepper.

- Serve with cold roast chicken or turkey.

Easy Creamy Dauphinoise

Serves 4–6 as an accompaniment

This is a delicious and versatile side dish for roast lamb, pork or even fish. You can also pop in a few fresh herbs or bacon bits.

600ml (1 pint) whipping cream

2 cloves garlic, crushed

800g (1 lb 12 oz) potatoes, peeled

salt and freshly ground black pepper

55g (2 oz) Gruyère cheese, grated, optional

- Preheat the oven to 200°C/400°F/Gas 6.

- Pour the cream into a pan, add the garlic and bring to the boil.

- Meanwhile, cut the potatoes lengthways into very thin slices – if you have one, a Japanese mandolin is perfect for this job.

- Season the potatoes all over and lay in a shallow ovenproof dish about 2–2½ litres (3½–4½ pints) capacity. Pour over the cream mixture and cook in the oven for 25–30 minutes, or until tender. If using, sprinkle the cheese over the top and return to the oven until just melting. Serve piping hot.

- If liked, you can allow the cooked potatoes to cool and spoon into ramekins. Sprinkle some of the cheese over the top of each, warm through in a microwave and quickly brown under a hot grill.

Roast Potatoes with Garlic, Smoked Bacon and Rosemary

Serves 4 as an accompaniment

Over the years I have cooked hundreds and hundreds of these roast potatoes. If you cook them at home the whole house is filled with the wonderful aroma of garlic and rosemary.

6–8 tbsp vegetable oil

450g (1 lb) King Edward or Desiree potatoes, peeled and cut into quarters

4 sprigs fresh rosemary

salt and freshly ground black pepper

6 rashers smoked streaky bacon, cut into thick strips

4 cloves garlic, crushed

- Preheat the oven to 160°C/325°F/Gas 3. Pour the oil into a non-stick roasting tin and place in the oven to heat.

- Place the potatoes in a pan and pour in enough cold water to cover. Bring the pan to the boil then reduce the heat and simmer for 2 minutes. Tip the potatoes into a colander and drain well.

- Add the potatoes to the roasting tin, together with the rosemary, and turn to coat in the oil. Season well and cook in the oven for about 40 minutes, or until the potatoes are brown and crispy on one side.

- Turn the potatoes over, sprinkle the bacon and garlic into the tin and mix well. Return the tin to the oven and continue cooking for a further 15–20 minutes, until the potatoes are golden. The potatoes will take on the flavours of the garlic and rosemary, and the bacon should be crisp. These are great served with any roast joint or even steaks.

Potato Scallops with Pickle

Serves 4 as an accompaniment

My dear grandmother used to cook these scallops as a treat for us when we were kids. Mum and Dad often went off to a show in Blackpool, and Grandma cooked potato scallops while she was babysitting. They're very tasty and go well with pickle or chutney.

2 large potatoes
1 small onion
vegetable oil, for deep-frying
300ml (½ pint) basic batter, see page 130
salt and freshly ground black pepper

- Wash and peel the potatoes, then cut them lengthways into slices about 2½mm (1/12 in) thick. Cut the onions into rings the same thickness as the potatoes.

- Heat the oil in a deep fat fryer to 180°C (350°F), or fill a deep saucepan one-third full with oil and heat, using a cooking thermometer to check the temperature.

- Make up the batter and allow to stand for 2–3 minutes, then beat again. Add a little more water if it has thickened up too much, but remember it needs to be thick enough to coat the potato slices.

- Sandwich a slice of onion between two potato slices, then carefully roll the edges of the scallop in the batter to coat, making sure you hold all the layers tightly together. Turn the scallop and coat in the batter completely.

- Cook the scallops in batter. Drop them into the hot oil and cook for about 4–5 minutes, carefully turning over halfway through the cooking. The scallops are ready when the batter is golden brown and crisp and the potato is cooked and tender.

- When cooked, remove from the oil and allow to drain on kitchen paper. Season well and serve with a pickle or chutney of your choice.

Boozy Food

Spiced Bloody Mary Soup

Serves 4

The only drink to have late on a Sunday morning is Bloody Mary. It should be very spicy and chilled, so the best thing to do is to make it the night before and chill overnight. Here, I've made it into a starter – it's quick and easy, and you can even pop it into a flask and take it on picnics.

> 100–125ml (3½–4 fl oz) vodka
> 2 × 400g cans chopped tomatoes in rich tomato sauce
> 3 tbsp lemon juice
> 1 tsp garam masala
> 4 tsp caster sugar
> 4 tbsp olive oil
> ½ tsp chilli powder
> 1½ tsp celery salt
> 1 tbsp Worcestershire sauce
> 1 small onion, finely chopped
> salt and freshly ground black pepper
> olive oil and celery leaves, to garnish

- Place all the ingredients in a liquidizer, together with 200ml (7 fl oz) of water, and blitz for a couple of minutes until smooth.

- Taste and check the seasoning, then chill well.

- Serve in bowls, drizzle a little olive oil over the surface and garnish with celery leaves.

Vodka and Stilton Croûtes

Serves 4–6 as light bites or canapés

Vodka and Stilton make a superb partnership – the vodka brings out the deep, full flavour of the Stilton. You will find that gin also works well in savoury dishes.

2½ tbsp olive oil

1 small onion, finely chopped

1 clove garlic, crushed

1 tbsp chopped fresh tarragon, plus extra sprigs to garnish

225g (8 oz) Stilton

2–3 tbsp vodka

2 ready-to-bake half baguettes, 150g (5½ oz) each

salt and freshly ground black pepper

- Preheat the oven to 180°C/350°F/Gas 4.

- Heat 1 tablespoon of the oil in a frying pan. Add the onion and garlic and cook gently until softened. Add the tarragon and cook for a further 2 minutes, then allow to cool.

- Crumble the Stilton in a small bowl, add the cooled onion mixture and season well, then add vodka to taste (the exact amount is up to you). Chill the mixture well in the fridge.

- Cut the bread on an angle into slices about 1½cm (⅝ in) thick and brush over the remaining olive oil. Season the bread well, place on a baking sheet in the preheated oven and cook, turning occasionally, for about 20 minutes, or until light golden and crisp. Remove from the heat and allow the bread to cool to room temperature.

- Spoon the chilled cheese mixture on to the bread, top with sprigs of tarragon and pile on to a plate.

Dry Sherry Marinade

This is a delicious marinade for chicken, duck and pork cutlets, but be careful when you are cooking the meat as the marinade can catch and burn easily because of the amount of sugar in it.

150ml (¼ pint) Chinese oyster sauce
50ml (2 fl oz) light soy sauce
125ml (4 fl oz) dry sherry
4 tsp ground cumin
2 tsp chilli powder
1 tsp lemon juice
125ml (4 fl oz) olive oil
8 tsp caster sugar
4 tsp garam masala
425g bottle Heinz tomato ketchup
salt and freshly ground black pepper

- Mix all the ingredients together in a large bowl and season. If covered, the marinade will keep well in the fridge for up to two weeks.

John Smith's Bitter Steak Marinade

Serves 4

I enjoy John Smith's beer so much that I decided to create a recipe that incorporates it. You could also use the marinade as the base for a beef stew, but it's perfect for steaks, especially when you are barbecuing them.

For the marinade:
440ml can John Smith's Smooth Bitter
2 tbsp Worcestershire sauce
8 tsp HP sauce
5 tsp wholegrain mustard
4 tsp honey
salt and freshly ground black pepper

4 lean rump steaks,
about 100g (3½ oz) each

- Place all the marinade ingredients in a large bowl, season and stir together. Allow to stand for 1 hour.

- Add the steaks to the mixture, make sure they are completely covered by the marinade and allow to marinate in the fridge for up to two days.

- When ready to cook, shake any excess marinade off the meat and pat dry using kitchen paper. Fry or grill the steaks.

- An alternative version of this recipe is to cook the steaks rare, then cool and chill them. Slice the chilled steaks thinly and serve with pickle and new potatoes.

Batters

As far as I'm concerned there is only one way to make batter, but other chefs use all sorts of ingredients to get a light, airy coating – yeast, egg whites, cornflour, etc. I can't recall exactly how I came across this method, but I do remember sitting next to my colleague Rick Stein at a lunch once and having a discussion about batters, during which he said he used lager. It's true that lager and self-raising flour make the *perfect* batter that works well with savoury or sweet dishes. It's very straightforward, provided you stick to a few simple rules.

225g (8 oz) self-raising flour
salt and freshly ground black pepper
300ml (½ pint) lager

- Sieve the flour into a bowl, season, then pour in the lager and whisk together slowly – do not overbeat. Add about 3 tablespoons of cold water. Allow to stand for 5–10 minutes, then check the consistency again (sometimes the batter thickens because of a chemical reaction in the flour, so you may need to add another splash of water).

- If the batter is allowed to stand for a couple of hours it will become heavy and leaden, so throw it away and make a fresh batch.

A few tips are:

- always dust food that is to be deep-fried in a little flour first, so that the batter will cling to it

- always cook in very hot oil

- drain foods well after deep-frying, do not cover and serve straightaway to stop the batter going soggy

- change the oil between frying savoury and sweet foods

Here are a few ideas for additions to the basic batter mixture:

- for a batter to use with fish, add ½ teaspoon of chilli powder and 25g (1 oz) of sesame seeds

- for a spicy batter for chicken add 1 tablespoon of chopped fresh parsley and 1 teaspoon of ground black pepper

- when deep-frying squid or prawns add 2 teaspoons of ground star anise to the batter

Dry Cider Jelly

Serves 4

This jelly is a wonderful summer pudding. The secret of good jellies is not to make them too firm – they are awful when hard like an ice hockey puck. The less gelatine used, the better. You can make port jelly in exactly the same way, simply replace the cider with port and omit the spices. It is, however, a bit more expensive.

3 sheets gelatine, about 10–15g
($\frac{1}{4}$–$\frac{1}{2}$ oz)
600ml (1 pint) dry strong cider
100g (3$\frac{1}{2}$ oz) caster sugar
1 tsp whole cloves
clotted cream, to serve

- Break the gelatine sheets into small pieces and place in a small bowl. Sprinkle over 3 tablespoons of the cider and allow to soak for 5–10 minutes until the gelatine has softened.

- Pour half the remaining cider into a pan, add the sugar and cloves and heat gently until the sugar dissolves, but do not allow to boil as this will drive off the alcohol. Bring to a simmer, then remove the pan from the heat, add the softened gelatine and stir until the gelatine has dissolved. Add the rest of the cider to the pan and allow to cool to room temperature.

- Strain the cooled jelly through a sieve into a shallow dish and chill in the fridge until set.

- Spoon the jelly into glasses and serve with clotted cream.

Spiced Christmas Punch

Serves 10–12

This is a good way to get Christmas Day off to a flying start. The most important thing is that the punch must not boil, as this 'drives off' the alcohol. Adjust the amount of sugar according to how much of a sweet tooth you have. Serve the punch warm rather than hot.

700ml (1¼ pints) dry red wine
700ml (1¼ pints) dry white wine
2 cinnamon sticks
15 whole cloves
2 oranges
2 lemons
about 225g (8 oz) caster sugar
10 allspice berries
10 black peppercorns
4 'breakfast tea' tea bags

- Place all the ingredients except the tea bags in a large pan and gently warm through until the sugar dissolves. Increase the heat and bring to just below boiling, stirring occasionally. Do not allow the liquid to boil. Add the tea bags and 300ml (½ pint) of cold water, then turn off the heat and cover the pan with a lid. Allow to stand for 10 minutes.

- Strain the punch through a sieve into a large jug and serve in glasses.

Pancakes

Basic Pancake Batter

Makes about 8 large or 12 small pancakes

I love pancakes, both sweet and savoury. The following recipes use this basic batter as their starting point. Enjoy!

2 eggs

100g (3½ oz) plain flour

about 300ml (½ pint) milk

25g (1 oz) butter, melted

vegetable oil, for frying

- Break the eggs into a bowl, add the flour and half the milk and whisk together until smooth, then whisk in the remaining milk and the melted butter to make a batter. You can add sugar to this basic mixture if the pancakes are going to be served sweet, or season with salt and pepper for savoury pancakes.

- Heat a frying pan until very hot, then add just a touch of oil and swirl it around. Continue heating until the oil begins to smoke, then pour in a little of the batter mixture and swirl the pan again so the mixture covers the pan base. Cook until the middle of the pancake is set, then check to make sure the underside is lightly browned and mottled. Turn over using a palette knife or fish slice and cook until the other side is just browned. Slide the cooked pancake on to a plate and repeat until all the remaining batter has been used.

- Stack the cooked pancakes on top of each other, then cover and seal the whole plate with clingfilm – the steam produced by the pancakes will stop them sticking together. They will keep like this in the fridge for 3–4 days.

Rolled Bacon Pancakes with Mustard and Parsley Cream

Serves 4

Bacon and parsley make an excellent pancake combination. They taste even better when served with mustard cream.

1 quantity basic pancake batter, see page 134

8 rashers smoked back bacon

300ml (½ pint) whipping cream

2 tsp white wine vinegar

pinch of caster sugar

¼–½ chicken stock cube, crumbled

2 tsp wholegrain mustard

salt and freshly ground black pepper

2 tbsp chopped fresh parsley

- Season the pancake batter with salt and pepper and cook as on page 134.

- Preheat the grill to high. Cook the bacon under the grill until crispy and golden, then cut into strips.

- Place the cream, vinegar, sugar, stock cube and mustard in a pan and bring to the boil. Season, then simmer rapidly until the cream reduces slightly and thickens. Stir in the parsley and season again.

- Gently warm the pancakes under the grill. Place the pancakes on plates, sprinkle over the bacon strips and roll each one up like a sausage. Pour over the mustard and parsley cream and serve.

Pancakes Stuffed with Cream Cheese and Spinach

Serves 4

My best mate, Paul, reckons he created this dish years ago when we worked in the Lakes together. The recipe is now on his menu at the brilliant Wig and Mitre in Lincoln. (If ever you go there you must also try Paul's strawberry tart – it has no match anywhere.)

25g (1 oz) pine nuts

½ quantity basic pancake batter, see page 134

vegetable oil, for frying

250g (9 oz) baby spinach

200g (7 oz) soft cream cheese

2 pinches freshly grated nutmeg

salt and freshly ground black pepper

Preheat the grill to medium. Place the pine nuts on a baking sheet and cook under the grill until golden brown, turning occasionally. Keep a close eye on them as they can catch and burn very easily.

Season the pancake batter and cook as described on page 134.

Cook the spinach in a large pan of boiling water for 2–3 minutes then drain into a colander and refresh under cold running water for another 2–3 minutes. Drain well again and squeeze out as much excess water as possible. Roughly chop the spinach and mix into the cream cheese. Add the pine nuts and nutmeg and season.

Lay a pancake on a plate and spoon some of the cream cheese mixture into the centre. Wrap it up like a parcel and fold under the ends. You can serve the pancakes cold, or just take the chill off them in a microwave, but take care not to make them too hot.

Fresh Strawberry Pancakes with Orange Custard Sauce

Serves 4

I think this is my favourite pancake dish – the combination of the strawberry and orange flavours is a very tasty one. At the hotel we jazz up this dish even more by glazing the pancakes with champagne sabayon and serving them with passionfruit sorbet.

500ml (18 fl oz) milk
1 vanilla pod, split
140g (5 oz) caster sugar
4 egg yolks
75g (2¾ oz) plain flour
1 quantity basic pancake batter, see page 134
450g (1 lb) ripe English strawberries, plus extra to serve
finely grated zest and juice of ½ orange
clotted cream, to serve

- Place the milk and vanilla pod in a pan and bring to the boil. Meanwhile, in a roomy bowl whisk together 125g (4½ oz) of the sugar and the egg yolks until pale and creamy, then add the flour and whisk in. Carefully pour the hot milk on to the mixture, stirring continuously.

- Return the mixture to a clean pan and stir over a low heat until it thickens and almost comes to the boil. Pour the custard into a bowl and place a piece of clingfilm directly on to the surface to stop a skin forming. Allow to cool.

- Add the remaining 15g (½ oz) of sugar to the pancake batter and mix well. Cook the pancakes as on page 134, then stack the cooked ones on top of each other and keep warm.

- Wash the strawberries one at a time and remove the stalks (always wash strawberries *before* you take out the stalks, otherwise they will fill with water and go soggy). Cut the strawberries in half and pop them into a mixing bowl.

- Add the orange juice and zest to the cooled custard and stir well, then add just enough of the custard to the strawberries to bind them.

- Spoon some of the strawberry custard mixture into the middle of each pancake and fold or roll up carefully – the mixture may be a little runny, but try not to let it run out of the edges.

- Place the pancakes on a plate (you can heat them for just a few seconds in a microwave if you want to take off the chill) and serve with the remaining custard, extra strawberries and clotted cream.

Lacy Pancakes with Chocolate Ice Cream and Bitter Chocolate Sauce

Serves 6

I was a judge on *Masterchef* a few years ago and a lady contestant came up with this pancake idea. Her pancakes were very good indeed so I've nicked the recipe. It's also a nice idea for the kids as it's a bit unusual.

1 quantity basic pancake batter, see page 134

55g (2 oz) cocoa powder

190g (6½ oz) caster sugar

15g (½ oz) unsalted butter, cut into small cubes

vegetable oil, for frying

12 scoops good quality chocolate ice cream

icing sugar, to dust

- Make up the pancake batter using slightly less milk than usual so it is just a bit thicker.

- Place 300ml (½ pint) of the water, the cocoa powder and 175g (6 oz) of the sugar in a pan and bring to the boil, whisking all the time. Allow to boil for 2 minutes, then remove from the heat and whisk in the butter. Keep warm.

- Heat a frying pan until very hot, then add a touch of oil, swirl it around and heat until just smoking. Stir the remaining sugar into the batter. Then, using a dessertspoon, drizzle some of the batter across the pan to make a lacy pattern a bit like a spider's web. When browned on the underside, turn over and cook the other side. Remove to a plate and keep warm. Repeat using the rest of the batter mixture.

- Stack a few pancakes on top of each other, add a couple of scoops of ice cream and drizzle over some of the chocolate sauce. Dust with icing sugar to finish.

139

Savoury Drop Scones with Cream Cheese, Smoked Salmon and Beets

Serves 4

Not a pancake, as you may have noticed, but another type of batter. This recipe is a very nice way of serving drop scones and it is easy to cook too. You can substitute the topping ingredients with cottage cheese and sliced smoked duck, or jam and clotted cream; they all work just as well.

150g (5½ oz) self-raising flour

1 tsp baking powder

1 egg

300ml (½ pint) milk

salt and freshly ground black pepper

200g (7 oz) cream cheese

½ tsp wholegrain mustard

lemon juice

2 tsp chopped fresh chives

225g (8 oz) sliced smoked salmon, cut into strips

a few sweet pickled baby beetroots, cut into slices

- In a bowl, mix together the flour, baking powder, egg and about a third of the milk and stir well to get rid of any lumps, then add enough of the remaining milk to make a thick batter. Season.

- Heat a non-stick frying pan, then add spoonfuls of the batter to make small round discs. Cook until just set, then flip over and cook the other side until browned – this will probably take about 3–4 minutes each side. Transfer the cooked drop scones on to a plate and cover with a clean tea-towel to keep them warm while you cook the remaining scones.

- Next, beat together the cream cheese and mustard until smooth, then add a squeeze of lemon juice, chives and season. You may want to add a splash of milk if the mixture feels too thick.

- To serve, spoon a little of the cream cheese on to each drop scone, top with some of the salmon and a slice of beetroot, then grind a generous amount of black pepper over the top.

Puds

Fresh Mango with Chilli Sugar

Serves 4

Somebody once told me there are 14,000 varieties of mango. I don't know if that is true or not, but either way, the mango is a delicious and succulent fruit which works very well with savoury foods like shellfish and chicken. Nevertheless, I still prefer it as a pud. It combines brilliantly with chilli and ice cream.

> 2 large ripe mangoes
> 55g (2 oz) icing sugar
> $\frac{1}{4}$ tsp hot chilli powder
> vanilla ice cream, to serve

- Preheat the grill to medium high.

- With a sharp knife, cut off both 'cheeks' of flesh from the mango, keeping the blade as close as possible to the flat central stone. Without going through the skin, make diagonal cuts through the cut face of the mango flesh, then make cuts across the other way so that you have a criss-cross effect. Pressing from the skin side, turn the mango halves inside out, so that you get a 'hedgehog' effect, but be careful not to tear the skin.

- Sieve the sugar and chilli powder together and mix thoroughly. Place the mango hedgehogs on a baking sheet and sprinkle equal amounts of the sugar mixture on to each. Place under the grill until the sugar caramelizes and turns golden brown – this will take 5–10 minutes. Remove from the grill and allow to cool for about 5 minutes.

- Serve on plates, spooning over any of the sugary juices that are left and topping with a large scoop of vanilla ice cream.

Ice Creams

I'm not going to begin to tell you how to make ice cream. It's a bit of a chore to put together and you really need the proper machine to do it well. So for the time being I'm going to show you the cheat's method.

There are plenty of premium brands of ice cream around and I urge you to buy these – they use the best ingredients and are well worth the extra expenditure. The secret to my cheat's ice cream is to buy a good base ice cream, like vanilla or chocolate, take it out of the freezer and slightly soften it in a bowl. It is very important that you do not allow it to melt. Then simply add your choice of flavourings and re-freeze. Here are a few ideas:

- stir roughly broken-up chocolate Hob Nob biscuits into vanilla ice cream to accompany cheesecakes

- stir cooled, melted chocolate into vanilla ice cream to make chocolate chip

- fold a chopped-up Crunchie bar into vanilla ice cream for a delicious accompaniment to strawberries

- soak raisins overnight in a little rum, then fold into vanilla ice cream to make rum and raisin

- fold chopped fresh basil into lemon ice cream for a great side dish to accompany strawberries and peaches

- crumble Christmas pudding into vanilla ice cream for a Christmas treat

Chilled Creamed Flaked Rice with Blueberries and Shortbread

Serves 4

I detested the rice pudding we had at school. Luckily, my mum made wonderful rice puddings, and we always used to fight over the baked skin. Needless to say, my dad always won, but then some things just aren't fair when you're a kid! Even Fern's kids seem to like this pud, so I must be doing something right.

600ml (1 pint) full-fat milk

1 vanilla pod, split

55g (2 oz) flaked rice

300g (10½ oz) crème fraîche

juice of ½ lemon

icing sugar, to taste

2 punnets blueberries

all butter shortbread biscuits, to serve

- Preheat the oven to 150°C/300°F/Gas 2.

- Heat the milk in a pan and bring to the boil, then add the vanilla pod. Stir in the rice, then pour the mixture into a shallow, ovenproof baking dish and cover with a piece of foil. Bake in the oven for 30–40 minutes until the rice is tender, creamy and thickened. Remove from the oven and leave to cool completely.

- When cool, spoon the thick rice pudding into a large bowl and remove the vanilla pod. Break it up using a spatula or fork, then add the crème fraîche, lemon juice and icing sugar to taste. Stir well and chill.

- To serve, spoon the rice pudding into big bowls and sprinkle over the blueberries. Serve with the shortbread biscuits.

Warm Raspberries with Fresh Limes and Double Cream

Serves 4

Raspberries are my favourite summer fruit. In my opinion, they are far superior to strawberries. This dish works best if you use slightly underripe berries which are a bit firmer. It is also very important to let them cool for 10 minutes to allow them to release the full flavour and taste. (Food should always be served neither too hot or too cold – otherwise the real flavour just doesn't come out.)

350g (12 oz) fresh raspberries

2 tbsp icing sugar

finely grated zest and juice of 2 limes

55g (2 oz) unsalted butter,
cut into small cubes

about 300ml (½ pint) double
cream, to serve

- Preheat the grill to high. Place the raspberries in a wide, heatproof flan dish so that they are in one or two layers. In a bowl, mix the icing sugar with the lime zest and juice and stir until dissolved, then pour the mixture over the raspberries.

- Dot the butter cubes evenly over the raspberries, then place the dish under the grill for 5–6 minutes, or until the raspberries are beginning to soften. Remove from the grill and allow to cool for about 10 minutes.

- Place the dish in the middle of the table and let people help themselves, passing a jug of cream around separately.

Chocolate Fudge Fondue with Marshmallows

Serves 4

This is a favourite with all children – quick, easy and very more-ish. I really enjoy making and eating this fondue, and it's excellent party food.

115g (4 oz) unsalted butter
190g (6½ oz) soft brown sugar
600ml (1 pint) double cream
½ lemon
115g (4 oz) dark bitter chocolate,
chopped into pieces
200g (7 oz) marshmallows

- Place the butter, sugar, cream and squeeze of lemon juice in a pan and heat until the sugar dissolves. Bring to the boil then reduce the heat and simmer for 2 minutes. Add the chocolate and stir until it has melted. Keep the fondue warm over a low heat.

- Stick long forks into the marshmallows and dip them in the chocolate.

Fresh Strawberries with White Wine Crush

Serves 4

Strawberries have been a huge disappointment to me in the past. Five or six years went by without my eating a decent one. So I decided to seek out someone who could grow the real thing rather than tasteless unripe mush. After a few months I found him – his strawberries are pure heaven. I phone him in the morning, he picks the strawberries fresh and delivers them in the evening; we even name the variety on the menu. The grower is a real find and I jealously guard his name and phone number.

If you can, try and pick your own strawberries. They are at their perfumed best after a couple of hot, sunny days. If you can't pick them yourself, go to the supermarket and smell the strawberries on display. Make sure they are fully ripe and look at the underside of the packet to check that they are not mushy or yellow. If you can resist, only eat strawberries in summer, otherwise you risk being disappointed.

115g (4 oz) icing sugar
350ml (12 fl oz) dry white wine
juice of 1 lemon and 1 lime
450g (1 lb) English strawberries

- Place the icing sugar and 150ml (¼ pint) of water in a pan and heat gently until the sugar dissolves. Allow to cool.

- Stir the wine, lemon and lime juices together with another 150ml (¼ pint) of water, into the cooled syrup, then pour into a plastic container and freeze overnight.

- To serve, make sure the strawberries are at room temperature then arrange in dishes. With a spoon, scrape the surface of the frozen crush and pile spoonfuls on top of the strawberries.

Rhubarb Fool

Serves 4

As kids, my brothers and I adored rhubarb and custard. Fortunately, my dad always seemed to have a plot full of it. I remember coming home from school to see two big bowls on the kitchen table – one full of thick, pale pink stewed rhubarb and the other full of thick Bird's custard with a skin on top. It's a classic combination.

675g (1½ lb) rhubarb
1 tbsp lemon juice
4 tbsp caster sugar, plus extra to taste
1 vanilla pod
300ml (½ pint) double cream
3 × 150g pots ready-made custard
shortbread, to serve

- Wash the rhubarb well, then chop into 2cm (¾ in) pieces and place in a pan. Add the lemon juice and sugar and cook over a low heat for about 25 minutes, stirring occasionally, or until the rhubarb has softened and cooked down. Don't be concerned that the pan is almost dry at the beginning – the water in the rhubarb will come out and cook down to give a deep-flavoured, thick compote. Allow to cool.

- Split the vanilla pod and scrape out the seeds. Whip the cream in a large bowl, together with the vanilla seeds, until the cream forms soft peaks, then add the custard and fold together. If you want to, you can add a little extra caster sugar to taste. Layer the cream mixture and rhubarb in dessert glasses and chill well. Serve with shortbread.

Sautéed Peaches with Lime, Madeira and Allspice

Serves 4

12 peach halves – canned 'cling' variety
or poached fresh peaches

1 vanilla pod, split

3 tbsp Madeira

juice of 1 lime

1 tsp ground allspice (Jamaican pepper)

115g (4 oz) light muscovado sugar

55g (2 oz) unsalted butter

250g (9 oz) mascarpone

- Dry the peaches well using kitchen paper or a clean tea-towel.

- Scrape the seeds out of the vanilla pod and place them in a pan with the Madeira, lime juice, allspice and muscovado sugar. Heat gently until the sugar has completely dissolved, but do not allow to boil. Keep warm on a low heat.

- In a large sauté or frying pan, heat the butter until it has melted, then increase the heat and cook until the butter is bubbling and beginning to brown. Add the peaches, cut side down, reduce heat slightly and sauté for about 2 minutes, or until golden brown. Turn the peaches over and cook for a further 1–2 minutes.

- Remove the sauté pan from the heat, pour in the Madeira mixture and swirl around gently. Add 1 tablespoon of mascarpone and stir in completely.

- To serve, divide the peach halves between four bowls and top with spoonfuls of the remaining mascarpone. Pour over the Madeira sauce and serve straightaway.

Deep-fried Bananas with Maple Syrup Custard

Serves 4

There are two ways to make custard: the proper, chef's way, using egg yolks, vanilla pods and milk, and the Bird's method. I love Bird's custard, it tastes delicious when it's made properly. I just add different ingredients to flavour the basic custard. Here, I've used maple syrup, but you can use golden syrup, lemon or orange oil, vanilla seeds . . . the possibilities are endless.

250g (9 oz) self-raising flour

3 tsp sesame seeds

2 pinches caster sugar, plus extra to sprinkle

300ml (½ pint) fizzy water

vegetable oil, for deep-frying

4 bananas, not too ripe

600ml (1 pint) custard

3–4 tbsp maple syrup

ground cinnamon, to dust

- In a bowl, mix 225g (8 oz) of the flour with the sesame seeds and 2 pinches of sugar, then whisk in enough fizzy water to make a batter. It should not be too thick, but it has to be able to coat the bananas. Allow to stand for 5 minutes.

- Meanwhile, heat the oil in a deep fat fryer to 180°C (350°F), or fill a deep saucepan one-third full with oil and heat. Peel the bananas, then cut each one into three pieces and lightly dust in the remaining flour. Dip the bananas in the batter to coat (if it has thickened up too much while standing, add a little extra water to thin it slightly), then drop them into the oil in batches, trying to keep them separate, and deep-fry for 4–5 minutes, or until golden brown and crisp. Drain well on kitchen paper.

- Heat the custard in a pan and add maple syrup to taste.

- Sprinkle caster sugar and a little cinnamon over the bananas. Pour the custard on to plates and pile the bananas on top.

Baked Apples with Pecans and Golden Syrup

Serves 4

This was the first pudding I made at college, so it's here partly for sentimental reasons, but also because it's so tasty. It's the perfect dish for a cold winter's day and the addition of golden syrup and pecans make it particularly delicious.

4 medium Bramley apples
(or, if you can get them, Howgate)

70g (2½ oz) pecan nuts

55g (2 oz) unsalted butter, cut into small cubes

4 tbsp golden syrup

600ml (1 pint) custard

- Preheat the oven to 200°C/400°F/Gas 6 and grease an ovenproof dish wide enough to take the apples in a single layer. Wash the apples well and remove the cores. To do this, press the corer halfway down through each apple, remove, then turn the apple over and push the corer right through the other end. Twist and take out the core. Using a sharp knife, make a cut just through the skin going completely around the widest part of the apples.

- Place the apples in the dish (they should fit quite snugly), and push half the pecans into the hollow centre of each apple. Add the butter cubes, then top up with the rest of the pecans and drizzle with the golden syrup. Bake in the oven for about 25 minutes, or until the apples just start to split and slightly puff up. They will look and smell delicious. Do not overcook. Remove from the oven and allow to cool for about 15–20 minutes, otherwise they will burn your mouth.

- Meanwhile, heat up the custard in a pan. Put the apples in individual, deep bowls, spoon over the buttery juices from the baking dish, and serve with lashings of custard.

Bob Vickery's Bread Pudding

This delicious pudding is my dad's recipe. He has always called it 'Wet Nelly', and to this day we don't know why! We often ate this as kids, served with custard with a skin on top – our favourite. If you add a little lemon juice to the custard, it gives it a wonderful flavour.

800g (1 lb 12 oz) loaf thick-sliced white bread

85g (3 oz) sultanas

85g (3 oz) currants

85g (3 oz) suet

2 eggs, beaten

2 tbsp black treacle

175g (6 oz) caster sugar, plus extra to sprinkle on top

2 tbsp ground mixed spice

2 tbsp marmalade

zest of 1 lemon, finely grated

custard, to serve

- Tear the bread into large pieces, leaving the crusts on. Place in a bowl and pour on enough cold water to cover. Allow to stand for 2 hours.

- After this time, preheat the oven to 180°C/350°F/Gas 4 and grease a tin measuring about 26 × 18cm (10½ × 7 in) and 5cm (2 in) deep.

- Squeeze out as much water as possible from the bread, then place the bread in a large bowl. In a separate bowl, add all the remaining ingredients and stir well. Add this mixture to the bread and mix together thoroughly. Pour into the greased baking tin and cook in the oven for about 50–60 minutes, or until set. Allow to cool, then sprinkle over a little caster sugar.

- To serve, cut into squares and, if you like, gently warm through in a microwave. Serve with lashings of custard.

Index

Page numbers in italic type refer to photographs